66- 73

The Civil War In Kentucky

LOWELL H. HARRISON

THE UNIVERSITY PRESS OF KENTUCKY

Research for The Kentucky Bicentennial Bookshelf
is assisted by a grant from the
National Endowment for the Humanities.
Views expressed in the Bookshelf do not
necessarily represent those of the Endowment.

ISBN: 0-8131-0209-X

Library of Congress Catalog Card Number: 75-3545

A statewide cooperative scholarly publishing agency
serving Berea College, Centre College of Kentucky,
Eastern Kentucky University, Georgetown College,
Kentucky Historical Society, Kentucky State University,
Morehead State University, Murray State University,
Northern Kentucky State College, Transylvania University,
University of Kentucky, University of Louisville, and
Western Kentucky University.

Editorial and Sales Offices: Lexington, Kentucky 40506

To my parents

Contents

Maps

Preface

THE CIVIL WAR was one of the most important events in American history. Although studied intensively for more than a century, it continues to fascinate and bewilder those who examine its myriad aspects. Even today there is no general agreement on why a country that prided itself upon its pragmatic politics could find no solution for its problems except a long and bloody fraternal war that cost more lives than any conflict in the nation's history. When that war came, Kentucky was truly a border state with strong attachments both north and south. In her anguish over the separation, Kentucky adopted a unique policy of neutrality that lasted for several months. When she did cast her fate with the Union cause, a group of her citizens formed a rival government that was admitted into the Confederacy. It is the purpose of this brief essay to review the struggle over secession and neutrality, to look at the course of the war within the commonwealth, and to suggest some of the effects the war had on the state and its citizens.

Two main considerations have established the limits of the survey. First, the compact format of the Bicentennial Bookshelf necessitates a great deal of generalization and summation and all too many omissions; it also precludes extensive documentation. Second, the subject of the survey is "The Civil War in Kentucky," not "Kentucky in the Civil War," which is a quite different and much broader topic. Only occasionally, therefore, have I ventured outside the boundaries of the commonwealth, although that limitation meant that I had to ignore the Civil War contributions of tens of thousands of Kentuckians who fought for the Union or the Confederacy far from their native state.

I have long been interested in the Civil War, and my research has extended over many years and into many libraries. The collections of the Kentucky Historical Society have been of great use, although during the preparation of this particular volume an extensive remodeling program has rendered them less accessible than in years past. I am especially grateful to the staffs of The Filson Club, the Louisville Free Public Library, the Special Collections of the Margaret I. King Library at the University of Kentucky, and the Kentucky Library at Western Kentucky University.

1

A STATE DIVIDED

As the sectional controversy moved along the path that led to secession and civil war, Kentucky occupied an extremely difficult position. Her citizens were sorely divided in their attitudes toward the problems for which the country was unable to find peaceful solutions. The public knew of family differences that divided such noted clans as the Breckinridges and the Clays; similar divisions split less well known families from the Jackson Purchase to the eastern mountains. Samuel McDowell Starling, a slaveholder from Hopkinsville, opposed secession so strongly that he volunteered for Union military service although he was past fifty years of age; he lost one son in Confederate service and another who died fighting for the Union. Such tragedies were repeated many times across the state.

Slavery was one of the institutions that bound Kentucky to the South. Slaves had been brought into the state since the early days of settlement, and in 1860 they constituted 19.5 percent of the population. But the percentage had been decreasing for several decades, and the state had few large slaveholders when measured by the standards of the Lower South. Many Kentuckians who cherished the Union saw nothing wrong with slavery.

A profitable trade association also bound Kentucky to

the states lying to the south. For many years the major outlet for her surplus produce had been the Mississippi River and its tributaries. The advent of railroads, however, created new commercial associations with the North that diminished the importance of the river traffic.

With the famed Kentucky Resolutions of 1798 and 1799 Kentucky had given the nation one of its first and most important expositions of the states' rights doctrine which, carried to its extreme, condoned the secession of a state from the Union. Yet her citizens had participated proudly in wars against Great Britain and Mexico, and most Kentuckians had endorsed the efforts of Henry Clay to find solutions to the controversies that threatened the existence of the nation they loved.

Sentimental ties to Virginia, from which Kentucky had been formed in 1792, and to North Carolina and Tennessee, each also the ancestral home of many Kentuckians, were strong. Yet these ties were countered by a new tug toward the free states, where tens of thousands of Kentucky's children lived by 1860.

Kentucky was relatively more important in 1860 than she has been in the twentieth century. Her population then ranked ninth in the nation, and she occupied seventh place in the value of farms and fifth in the value of livestock. Her diversified agriculture supplied vast quantities of tobacco, corn, wheat, hemp, and flax; and the superiority of Bluegrass whiskey was generally recognized, regardless of other sectional disputes. Manufacturing lagged well behind agriculture in the state's economy, but in 1860 Kentucky ranked fifteenth in both capital invested in manufacturing and the annual value of products; she was thirteenth in the cost of raw materials used in her industries.[1]

The state's geographical location was of great strategic importance. Her accession to the South would give the Confederacy a defensible river boundary and one along which Confederate armies would pose the threat of a drive to the Great Lakes that could split the Union. No one recognized this significance of the commonwealth more clearly than Abraham Lincoln. "I think to lose Kentucky is nearly the same as to lose the whole game," he wrote a friend in September 1861. "Kentucky gone, we cannot hold Missouri, nor, as I think, Maryland. These all against us, and the job on our hands is too large for us. We would as well consent to separation at once, including the surrender of the capital." [2]

The nation had been moving toward the hour of crisis for many years. The Compromise of 1850, which Kentucky's Henry Clay helped formulate, had failed to resolve the sectional differences. Indeed, the struggle had intensified after the passage of the Kansas-Nebraska Act in 1854 and the birth of the Republican party, which had no southern wing to help force a moderate course upon it. While the sectional struggle had many facets, the focal point had come to be the future of slavery in the territories. A variety of observers agreed that slavery had to be able to expand or it would ultimately die, much like a grass fire that burns itself out when prevented from spreading. Both friends and foes of slavery fought to control the future of the institution in such areas as Kansas, where a small-scale civil war preceded the greater conflict. The Supreme Court's effort to solve the issue in the Dred Scott decision of 1857 had failed. Antislavery forces would not accept as final the Court's proslavery stance, and the defenders of slavery were even less inclined to accept compromise after the Court had endorsed their contentions.

The political problems that beset Kentucky were complicated during the 1850s by the dissolution of the Whig party, which had long dominated the state's politics. Despite the efforts of such Kentuckians as Cassius M. Clay, the new Republican party made little progress within the state, although John C. Frémont, the party's first presidential candidate, had done surprisingly well in the North in the 1856 presidential election. During the last years of the decade Kentucky politics were even more confused than usual. Some of the old Whigs became reluctant Democrats, a few joined the Republicans, and many voted Native American or Know-Nothing for a time. As the nation approached the 1860 election, the two major political groups in the state were the Democrats, who had become the majority party, and the Constitutionalists, who shared a somewhat pathetic hope that repeated reference to the sanctity of the Constitution and the Union would somehow solve the problems confronting the state and the nation.

Such hopes were shattered by the events of 1860. When the Democratic party split along sectional lines, one of the last political bonds holding the nation together disappeared. John C. Breckinridge, vice president of the United States and one of Kentucky's greatest orators, was nominated for the presidency by the Southern Democrats; Stephen A. Douglas, the "Little Giant" of Illinois, became the candidate of the Northern Democrats. Kentuckians found little solace in the nomination of Lincoln by the Republicans. He was a native of Kentucky, but his "house divided" speech had alarmed many slaveholders who would not accept the curtailment of slavery expansion that he and his party demanded. As the campaign progressed, many Kentuckians turned toward John Bell, the Constitutional Union candidate from neighboring Tennessee, whose simple platform was the preservation of the Union.

Bell captured a majority in 35 of Kentucky's 110 counties in 1860 and won a plurality in 25 more. He was strongest in the old Whig strongholds and in the counties where the largest slaveholders were grouped. Breckinridge had a majority in 36 counties but pluralities in only 7; despite his Southern affiliation, he failed to carry most of the counties with the heaviest concentration of slaves. Douglas had a majority in only 7 counties, and Lincoln did not carry a single one. The popular vote was 66,051 for Bell, 53,143 for Breckinridge, 25,638 for Douglas, and 1,364 for Lincoln. Although Fayette County contained a number of Lincoln's in-laws, he received just five votes there.[3] But Lincoln swept most of the northern states, and with just less than 40 percent of the popular vote he received a clear majority of the electoral ballots.

Several weeks before the election George D. Prentice, the editor of the Louisville *Daily Journal,* had remarked hopefully that the public usually quieted down after a bitter election. But, he warned, "for the first time in the history of our country, this calm after the storm is imperilled; we are threatened even now by the angry mutterings of an impending storm, which, as some think portends—disaster and devastation." The editor had attempted to prevent Lincoln's election, but he was not totally dismayed by the result. The Republicans would not control either Congress or the courts, and impeachment could be employed if Lincoln exceeded his lawful powers. "He could not infringe the Constitution if he would," Prentice declared. While he blamed "the ignorance and fanaticism of the Abolition party" for the crisis, Prentice denied that the Republicans were the abolition party.[4]

Many Southerners, including numerous Kentuckians, did not agree with Prentice. The election of a sectional president by a sectional party committed to halting the expansion of slavery was, to them, a call for action. Perhaps the incoming administration could not harm the South at that moment, but why should sovereign states wait until they were injured before defending themselves? The states' rights doctrine, expressed in the Kentucky Resolutions and honed into precision by such great Southern leaders as the late John C. Calhoun, asserted that a state could, if need be, protect itself against the tyranny of the majority by withdrawing from the Union. Such a move would not constitute rebellion or insurrection; it was the exercise of a basic constitutional right. The federal government, the agent of the states, had no right to prevent a state from following such a course of action.

Led by South Carolina, whose convention approved secession unanimously on December 20, 1860, the states of the Lower South began the process that led to the formation of the Confederate States of America. Some advocates of secession did not view it as a step toward a permanent separation. "We can make better terms out of the Union than in it," predicted Thomas R. R. Cobb of Georgia, and some Kentuckians agreed with him. Obviously, the more extensive the secession movement, the more pressure it would place on the federal government to make sweeping concessions. But eight of the fifteen slave states held back from the first wave of secession, and Kentucky was one of that number.

"No one believes that Kentucky as a state is for disunion or secession," Charles A. Wickliffe insisted to a friend only days after Lincoln's election. Wickliffe wanted "a grand Mass Convention of all Kentuckians opposed to the present division movement . . . to proclaim to the Country that Kentucky will stand by the Union, or perish with it." [5] His sentiments were echoed at numerous town and county meetings and in the editorial columns of much of the state's press. On December 18 Senator John J. Crittenden, Clay's successor in the role of compromiser, revealed a detailed, comprehensive plan designed to resolve the crisis, and Kentucky participated anxiously, hopefully, and unsuccessfully in this and other efforts at compromise. All of them collapsed on the issue of the expansion of slavery.

Beriah Magoffin, the Democrat who had been elected governor in 1859, bore much of the burden of trying to chart the course of the state during the crisis. He was a firm defender of slavery. "I do not believe slavery to be wrong," he had told the legislature; "I do not believe it to be a moral, social, or political evil." He also supported the right of secession, and he was convinced that Southern rights had been violated. But he was opposed to immediate secession, and in an effort to prevent it he sent a circular letter to the other slave-state governors on December 9, 1860. The minimum demands of the South, he suggested, should include strict enforcement of the fugitive slave act, the division of the common territories at the 37th parallel, a perpetual guarantee of the free use of the Mississippi River, and some sort of Southern veto in the Senate over slavery legislation. These rights could be secured, the governor declared, by holding first a conference of all the slave states, followed by a full conference of all the states in the Union.[6]

Before the end of the month the governor restated his position in response to a plea from Alabama that Kentucky, "who so gallantly vindicated the sovereignty of the States in 1798," join the secession movement already under way. Kentucky shared the South's outrage over the injustices committed by the North, Magoffin replied, but he favored, instead of secession, a conference of slave states to formulate united demands to the North. "You have no hope of a redress in the Union," the governor wrote. "We yet look hopefully to assurances that a powerful reaction is going on at the North."[7]

On December 27 the governor called a special session of the legislature to consider the situation confronting the commonwealth. It was already too late for the Southern conference he had sought, Magoffin told the legislators; Kentucky should therefore hold her own convention to decide upon her own course of action. Meanwhile, in a last effort "to save the old ship" from wrecking "upon the rocks of disunion," Kentucky should participate in the conference of border states scheduled for early February. The Frankfort *Tri-Weekly Commonwealth* examined Magoffin's request for a convention and concluded that "the Governor of Kentucky is a secessionist," a sentiment shared by many of his constituents.[8] The legislature rejected Magoffin's proposed convention, but it sent six delegates to the futile Peace Conference that convened in Washington on February 4, and it asked Congress to call a national convention to consider amendments such as those Crittenden had proposed.

The legislature adjourned from February 11 until March 20. When it reconvened, the members called for a border state convention to meet in Frankfort on May 27. It also ratified a proposed thirteenth amendment to the Constitution that would have guaranteed slavery in the states where it was legal. The session ended in early April, a week before the Civil War opened with the bombardment of Fort Sumter.

As the war started, many Kentuckians shared both Magoffin's opposition to secession and his conviction that the Union should not be held together by force. When Kentucky was asked to supply four regiments as its quota of the 75,000 volunteers called for by the president, Magoffin refused to cooperate: "I say, emphatically, Kentucky will furnish no troops for the wicked purpose of subduing her sister Southern States." [9] But Kentucky also refused to join the second wave of secession that carried North Carolina, Tennessee, Virginia, and Arkansas out of the Union and into the Confederacy. Some extreme Southern Rightists demanded immediate secession, and some extreme Unionists wanted to help stamp out rebellion, but the majority of Kentuckians favored the unusual policy of neutrality that was finally adopted. The revered Crittenden spoke for the mass of his constituents when he declared on April 17 that Kentucky's proper role was that of a mediator between the two hostile forces, and on April 30 he wrote a son: "Kentucky has not seceded, and I believe never will. She loves the Union and will cling to it as long as possible. And so, I hope, will you. . . . God knows what is to be the end." [10] Unionist meetings, composed largely of Bell and Douglas supporters of 1860, endorsed a neutral role while condemning both secession and coercion. Prentice expressed their hopes in the March 20 issue of his *Journal* when he proclaimed: "KENTUCKIANS! YOU CONSTITUTE TODAY THE FORLORN HOPE OF THE UNION."

While Magoffin's sympathies were with the Confederacy, he feared a Union invasion if Kentucky should move in that direction, and many of his fellow citizens were opposed to secession. A convention during the secession excitement might have succeeded in sweeping Kentucky out of the Union, but the Southern Rightists were unable to secure the call. Lincoln sensed the delicacy of the situation and, without relinquishing any principle of Unionism, let it be known that he would not, for the time being, challenge the state's neutrality. On May 16 by a vote of 69-29 the Kentucky House of Representatives resolved: "That this state and the citizens thereof shall take no part in the Civil War now being waged, except as mediators and friends to the belligerent parties; and that Kentucky should, during the contest, occupy a position of strict neutrality." The Senate later adopted a somewhat similar resolution, and the governor proclaimed the state's neutrality on May 20. A bewildered observer from abroad might well have concluded that the United States had become three countries: the Union, the Confederacy, and Kentucky.

Few Kentuckians with political acumen could have expected neutrality to continue permanently. The vital questions were: When would it end? And in what direction would the commonwealth move next? While both factions made every effort to influence the final decision, for several months the state's unique status continued in precarious balance. But volunteers slipped away to join the armies that were being raised, and some covert recruiting occurred within the state. In an unusual effort to find some solution, the Unionists selected Crittenden, Archibald Dixon, and S. S. Nicholas to treat with Magoffin, John C. Breckinridge, and Richard Hawes, the spokesmen for the Southern Rightists.

9

The sextet agreed to continue neutrality and to make provisions for the state's defense, but their cooperation broke down when the Unionists refused to accept the governor as a member of a special five-man board that would be in charge of the state's military preparedness.

When the legislature finally established such a board on May 24, it was given the supervisory military functions lodged in the governor by the state's constitution. During the period of strained neutrality each faction organized its own military force. Inspector General Simon B. Buckner's State Guards were largely Confederate in sentiment; the new Home Guards were overwhelmingly Unionist. Both forces engaged in a feverish search for weapons and in sporadic drilling. Naval Lieutenant William "Bull" Nelson, whose vast bulk made him one of the most improbable undercover agents of the war, was instrumental in shipping 5,000 "Lincoln guns" into the state, where staunch Union men connived in their distribution. James M. Shackleford of Richmond, for example, wrote Nelson to see "whether we can get 100 Enfield or Sharps rifles, we are organizing two Companies of everlasting Union men, in our town and county and want this description of arms for one of them." [11] The Southern Rightists were equally guilty in intent but less successful in securing weapons. Several times clashes were narrowly avoided, and there was grave danger that a chance encounter would touch off civil war within the state. But General Buckner negotiated agreements in June with Union General George B. McClellan and Governor Isham Harris of Tennessee whereby both agreed to respect the state's neutrality, and, somehow, the fragile policy survived through the humid months of a Kentucky summer.

Two elections held during the summer of 1861 indicated the relative strength of the two groups and foreshadowed the commonwealth's ultimate decision. The Unionists, spurred on by the efforts of such radicals as Joseph Holt, made strenuous efforts to sweep the congressional election of June 20. Especially effective against the Southern Rightists were their charges that the Confederacy would destroy the lucrative market for Kentucky's surplus slaves by reopening the foreign slave trade and that the South "only wants Kentucky to stand between her & danger, to be her battleground." [12] Recognizing that defeat was certain, many Southern Rightists boycotted the election. The total vote was just over half the 1860 canvass, and the Unionists won nine of ten seats. The Southern Rightists carried only the First District in the extreme western end of the state, as the Unionists achieved a 54,700 majority in the 125,000 ballots cast.

The Unionists won another decisive political battle on August 5, when state legislators were elected. Earlier in the year confident Southern Rightists had expected to win control of the legislature, after which they would order a convention that would pass the ordinance of secession. But their prospects had dimmed, and again many Southern advocates stayed away from the polls. The new legislature had a 76-24 Unionist majority in the house and a 27-11 margin in the senate, although only half the senate seats had been up for election. These figures may not have been an accurate gauge of public sentiment, but they provided margins sufficient to override gubernatorial vetoes. The tide was flowing toward the Union, and the neutrality policy was soon subjected to increased strains.

Much of the Union recruiting of Kentuckians had been carried on from camps just north of the Ohio River, although Nelson had been active in the Crab Orchard area since early July. As soon as the results of the August election were known, he established Camp Dick Robinson in Garrard County, to the dismay of many moderate Unionists who continued to view neutrality as the best policy for the commonwealth. When Crittenden voiced such discontent, Nelson replied blandly, "That a camp of loyal Union men, native Kentuckians, should

11

assemble in camp under the flag of the Union and upon their native soil [and] should be a cause of apprehension is something I do not clearly understand." Magoffin received a similar rebuff when he protested the breach of neutrality to President Lincoln. The president, pointing out the governor's failure to "entertain any desire for the preservation of the Federal Union," refused to close the camp and to halt enlistments. "Taking all the means within my reach to form a judgment," Lincoln wrote, "I do not believe it is the popular wish of Kentucky that this force shall be removed beyond her limits; and, with this impression, I must respectfully decline to so remove it." [13] Confederate authorities were more circumspect in their activities, but they were in contact with Kentucky officials and citizens sympathetic to their cause, and Camp Boone, just inside the Tennessee border a few miles south of Guthrie, received a steady stream of Kentucky volunteers.

By late August the Confederate supporters had become the state's strongest advocates of continued neutrality. The secessionist movement no longer had any prospect of success, and if Kentucky relinquished her neutrality, it would be to join the Union. Incidents became more frequent and bitter, but an open rupture was avoided until early September, when the decisive event occurred in the western end of the state. Both sides recognized the strategic importance of controlling the Mississippi, Tennessee, and Cumberland rivers; and such river ports as Columbus, Paducah, and Smithland assumed unwonted importance. The impetuous Confederate General Gideon Pillow had wanted to seize Columbus as early as May, but he had been dissuaded by Buckner. In early September, General Leonidas Polk, the Episcopal bishop who held the command in western Tennessee, became convinced that Federal troops were poised to make the move and ordered Pillow to occupy Columbus. Pillow did so on

September 4, and Union forces commanded by Ulysses S. Grant then seized Paducah.

Governor Magoffin denounced both sides for "equally palpable and open violations of the neutral rights of Kentucky," and he demanded that all military forces be withdrawn at once. But the Unionist majorities in the legislature rejected a resolution to that effect; instead, they demanded a unilateral Confederate withdrawal. When the governor vetoed their resolution, he was overridden by 68-26 and 25-9 margins in the house and senate.[14] Desperate last-minute efforts to restore Kentucky's neutrality failed, and the state at last found itself at its Rubicon. The delay had been of value, for it had allowed time for the dominant opinion to organize and make itself heard. As the Civil War came to Kentucky in the late summer of 1861, there was no doubt but that the prevailing sentiment in the state was Unionist.

2

THE WAR BEGINS

With the end of Kentucky's neutrality, Union and Confederate troops poured into the state as each side sought to control as much territory as possible. On September 18 the legislature called for the expulsion of the Confederates and gave command of the state volunteers to General Robert Anderson, the Kentuckian who had won fame by his defense of Fort Sumter. Thomas L. Crittenden was put in charge of the reorganized State Guard, Buckner having refused a Union commission. Anderson established his headquarters in Louisville, through which troops and supplies were pouring for the state's defense. Never in good health after his South Carolina ordeal, Anderson relinquished command on October 8 to General William T. Sherman. George H. Thomas, a Virginian who had refused to follow his state into secession, commanded at Camp Dick Robinson, while Nelson, having made a quick switch from naval lieutenant to army brigadier general, opened Camp Kenton near Maysville. In the western end of the state Grant commanded the forces that had seized Smithland and Paducah.

Sherman soon found himself in difficulties with his superiors when he took a realistic view of what would be required to win the war. He was disappointed by the reaction of Kentuckians, who had been expected to sweep away all traces of secession and provide a major increment to the Union's war effort. To the contrary, Sherman complained, "the Kentuckians, instead of assisting, call from every quarter for protection against local secessionists." Adjutant General Lorenzo Thomas, after conferring with Sherman in Louisville on October 16, reported Sherman's complaint that "the young men were generally secessionists and had joined the Confederates, while the Union men, the aged and conservatives, would not enroll themselves to engage in conflict with their relations on the other side." [1] Competing Union and state authorities had authorized the raising of too many units; would-be officers abounded, but too few recruits were content to serve in the ranks. By the end of 1861 some 29,203 Kentuckians had been accepted into Union service; 42,000 had been sought.

Military equipment was in such short supply that many of the new troops could not even be armed with rifles. Sherman had no defense line for his scattered forces, and he was convinced that they were in imminent danger of being overwhelmed by massive Confederate armies. He needed 200,000 men, he declared, a figure that caused his superiors to question both his judgment and his nerve. Secretary of War Simon Cameron telegraphed President Lincoln from Louisville in mid-October: "Matters are in a much worse condition than I expected to find them. A large number of troops needed here immediately." [2] But Sherman was held responsible for much of the situation, and the following month Don Carlos Buell replaced him as commander of the Army of the Ohio.

The Unionists hastened the departure of many Confederates from the state. Some Kentuckians had left to join the Southern army within days of the fall of Fort Sumter, but the Confederacy had not pushed for enlistments, partly because of the acute shortage of equipment and partly because of the state's neutrality. The number leaving the state increased after Camp Boone was established, and it spurted after the events of early September, despite Union efforts to apprehend suspected Confederate sympathizers. John Hunt Morgan, for example, slipped away from Lexington on the night of September 20, taking with him members of the elite Kentucky Rifles, and Senator Breckinridge, former vice-president of the United States, eluded capture by fleeing to Virginia, where he accepted a commission in the Conferate army. Breckinridge would not see his home again for nearly eight years, a record matched by few other Kentucky Confederates. Such distinguished citizens as ex-Governor Charles S. Morehead and R. T. Durrett were seized and shipped to Northern prisons.

On September 10, 1861, General Albert Sidney Johnston was placed in command of Confederate Department No. 2, a military monstrosity that stretched all the way from the Appalachian Mountains in the east to the Indian Territory in the west. Born in Washington, Kentucky, Johnston had distinguished himself in the armies of both the United States and the Republic of Texas. During the 1850s he had commanded the famed Second U.S. Cavalry in which Robert E. Lee had served as lieutenant colonel. Head of the Department of the Pacific when the war started, Johnston resigned his commission and made the long, dangerous trip cross-continent to Richmond, where he became one of the Confederacy's full generals. He enjoyed the complete confidence of President Jefferson Davis, who later rejected a demand for his removal by declaring, "If Sidney Johnston is not a general . . . we have no general." [3]

As soon as Johnston assumed command at Nashville he appointed Buckner brigadier general and ordered him to occupy Bowling Green. This advance would help straighten the Confederate line and protect the rich supplies of northern Tennessee; it might also gain both men and supplies from southern Kentucky while denying them to the enemy. Buckner entrained on the Louisville and Nashville Railroad on September 17 and reached Bowling Green the next morning with a vanguard of some 1,300 men. The anticipated arrival of the Confederates had already created consternation among the town's Union population. "Some of the members have sold out and gone," a local woman wrote. "And they have been moving the women and children out of town all the week and some of them are almost frightened to death. . . . It seems evident that Bowling Green is a doomed city." A Confederate officer, surprised at the extent of Unionist support in the southern part of the state, reported, "One old woman met us with a Bible in her hand, said she was prepared to die." [4]

Most of the troops in the Bowling Green area camped along the Barren River, where wood and water were plentiful. In addition to holding intensive drill sessions, they labored on massive fortifications designed to foil the anticipated Federal assault. A Union officer who inspected the Confederate works in February 1862 after the evacuation of Bowling Green could hardly believe that "the Southern army could have completed such vast works. The labor has been immense—their troops cannot be well drilled—their time must have been chiefly spent in hard work, with the axe and spade." [5]

The arrival of General Johnston in late October indicated the importance he attached to the position. By January 1862 he had only 48,000 men to defend a front that stretched nearly 400 miles across the southern portion of the state. His major concentrations were at Cumberland Gap, Bowling Green, Forts Henry and Donelson in Tennessee, and Columbus. The department was also short of most supplies and equipment, and Johnston spent much of his time appealing to state and Confederate officials for additional help. Like his Union counterpart, Johnston was initially disappointed by the number of Kentucky volunteers. "There are thousands of ardent friends to the South in the state," he wrote Secretary of War Judah P. Benjamin, "but there is apparently among them no concert of action." [6] When the

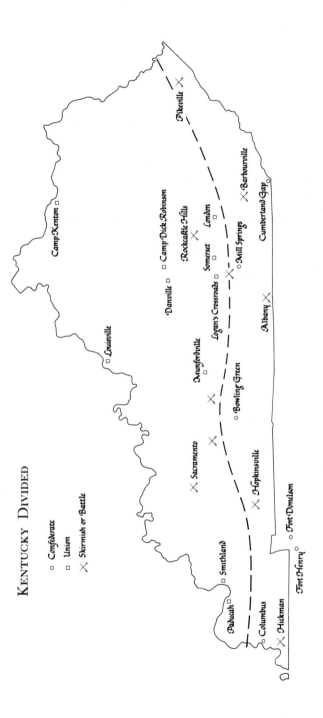

KENTUCKY DIVIDED

○ Confederate
□ Union
✕ Skirmish or Battle

number of volunteers increased to a more satisfactory figure, General Johnston was embarrassed by his inability to equip them.

Each army in Kentucky grossly overestimated the strength of the other, and each worked frantically to prepare for an attack by its supposedly more numerous foe. A great deal of activity occurred during the last months of 1861, particularly along the Green River. Both Union and Confederate recruits received some badly needed field experience in marches and forays calculated to gain intelligence about the enemy and to deny him any knowledge of what his opponent was doing. Camp rumors foretold a major battle along the Green River, but the rain-drenched autumn passed without the predicted clash. Yet the war gradually became more real, for civilians as well as for the new soldiers, some of whom were already regretting their eagerness to enlist. The romance of war meant little to Mary H. Wallace when she stood by the road and watched a Confederate column tramp by on its way to Hopkinsville. "I saw Brother pass by without being able even to shake hands & when he disappeared amid the dust noise & confusion of sounds attendant on a march I felt as if I would never see him again. I put my face down on the gate & cried with all my heart." [7]

The first shot of the Civil War in Kentucky was reported fired in at least a dozen different places, but the few engagements that occurred in late 1861 were on a scale that would appear insignificant when measured against later conflicts. Among the few skirmishes of consequence was the October 21 action in the Rockcastle Hills in the southeastern part of the state. General Felix Zollicoffer, attempting to thrust beyond London into central Kentucky, was checked by a well-fortified Union force under the command of Brigadier General Albin Schoepf. Combined casualties were probably under 100; but when Zollicoffer withdrew, Unionist boasts escalated the affair into a major victory. Another Union force encountered Nathan B. Forrest, an untutored military genius, at Sacramento on December 28, and the survivors contributed to the building of the Forrest legend. More than a score of other Kentucky communities also experienced their first taste of the war during the closing months of 1861.

While the armies sought inconclusively for an advantage, the Confederates in southern Kentucky moved to establish the proper constitutional relationship with the Confederate States of America. Aware that the Frankfort government was hopelessly Unionist, such Confederate leaders as George W. Johnson of Scott County and General John C. Breckinridge decided to establish a government that would reflect their views. A preliminary meeting held in Russellville on October 29–30 condemned the Frankfort legislature for its many crimes and appealed to the fundamental right of the people "to alter, reform, or abolish their government, in such manner as they think proper." Assuming that Governor Magoffin could not provide for a meeting of the legislature free from the intimidation of Federal troops, the secessionist representatives from 32 counties established a committee to arrange for a sovereignty convention.

Some 115 delegates from 68 counties assembled in Russellville on November 18, but many were soldiers or civilians who had fled to the protection of the army at Bowling Green. They were somewhat embarrassed by having to violate a portion of the cherished doctrine of states' rights, but the state legislature would hardly call the special convention that could pass an ordinance of secession. So the convention, presided over by Henry C. Burnett of Trigg County, appealed to "the ultimate right of revolution possessed by all mankind against perfidious and despotic government" for justification of its actions. Since "the President and Congress have treated this supreme law of the Union with contempt, and usurped to themselves the right to interfere with the rights and liberties of the States and the people,"

command, he could do little to remedy Zollicoffer's situation.

Given more favorable conditions, Zollicoffer hoped to advance against Danville or London. Meanwhile, to assist in his probing reconnaissance and to facilitate a rapid movement against the Federal forces, he moved to the north side of the Cumberland, despite the danger of being confronted by a larger enemy army while a river subject to sudden floods cut across his line of retreat. Expected reinforcements were detained in Tennessee, supplies continued to be inadequate, and General Johnston provided little guidance for the developing crisis on his right flank. President Davis complicated the situation by appointing George B. Crittenden, a son of the senator, to command and relegating Zollicoffer to head the army's First Brigade.

By January 1862, when Crittenden arrived to assume command, Thomas's army had become so much stronger that the best chance of success for the Confederates lay in holding their defensive positions until Thomas came to them. Crittenden was disturbed that Zollicoffer had not pulled the Confederate troops back across the Cumberland River to its south bank. But he agreed that with the waters almost at flood stage, the withdrawal would have to be postponed. Little time remained to him, however, for the Union army had finally begun its advance.

Thomas had wanted to cut the Confederates' supply line, perhaps by seizing control of the river at Burkesville, but Buell ordered him to move eastward and concentrate with Schoepf near Somerset. The army moved slowly over roads no better than quagmires; the infantry averaged only five miles a day, and the artillery and supply wagons could not keep up with them. By January 17 Thomas was at Logan's Crossroads, still several miles from Somerset and some nine or ten miles north of the Confederate fortifications. Since his rearguard was lagging far behind, Thomas ordered Schoepf to come to him so that they could attempt to carry out Buell's order to capture or disperse the Confederate force.[11]

Crittenden knew of Thomas's approach, but he thought that swollen streams would prevent Schoepf from joining Thomas for at least a day or two. Although they had only 4,000 effectives, Crittenden proposed to a council of war on Saturday evening, January 18, that they attack Thomas before he was reinforced. Zollicoffer may have objected, but the Confederates started their advance soon after midnight. A cold rain began to fall, and progress was painfully slow in the wintry darkness. The troops were wet, hungry, and weary when the crackle of gunfire signaled contact with the enemy. It was then a little short of seven o'clock on Sunday morning, January 19.

The Tenth Indiana Infantry and Colonel Speed F. Fry's Fourth Kentucky Infantry regiments withstood the early Confederate assault until Thomas could get up reinforcements. When Confederates fired on his men from the shelter of a ravine, Fry became so incensed that he climbed a rail fence and "defied them to stand up and fight like men." The usual battlefield confusion was augmented by a dense pall of rain, smoke, and fog and by thick timber and undergrowth that rendered artillery almost useless and compounded the commanders' problems of controlling their troops. During the early-morning confusion General Zollicoffer rode into the Union lines. He thought he was among Confederate units, and his raincoat concealed his own identity. "We are firing on our own men!" he told Colonel Fry, and the latter was giving the order to cease fire when a Confederate staff officer galloped up and yelled, "It's the enemy, General!" General Zollicoffer was immediately shot out of the saddle.[12]

Disheartened by the news, some Confederates began to drift away from the fighting, but a savage charge by the Twentieth Tennessee and Fifteenth Alabama regiments temporarily stabilized the line. Thomas, personally directing his units as they went into action, checked the Confederates at the rail fence that had been Fry's pulpit. The men fought viciously at such close range that some seized rifles across the fence and attempted to wrestle them away from their owners. Thomas poured in more troops, and he was finally able to get some artillery into action. About ten o'clock, some three hours after the first shots, the Confederate left was broken. Despite heavy casualties, the Mississippi and Tennessee regiments that had already fought so gallantly protected the retreat and prevented a disaster. Both sides had used about 4,000 men. The Confederate losses were reported as 125 killed, 309 wounded, and 95 missing; the Union casualties were 40 killed, 207 wounded, and 15 missing.

Two fresh Union regiments pushed the pursuit, and by late afternoon some of Thomas's artillery was firing on the main rebel fortifications just north of the river at Beech Grove. Since he thought it too late for an assault, Thomas made careful preparations for an early morning advance. But Crittenden, realizing that the fortifications on the north side of the river were untenable, decided to evacuate the ill-chosen position. During a hectic night the *Noble Ellis,* a little stern-wheeler, transferred most of the troops across the flooded stream. Panic developed as daybreak neared. Some soldiers had to be beaten off the overloaded vessel, and a number of others drowned trying to swim across the river. Supplies, artillery, horses, the wounded—Crittenden had to abandon most of them. As he retreated to Gainesboro, Tennessee, to reorganize, Crittenden's army dwindled sharply as both men and officers deserted. Since the dead Zollicoffer had become a hero, Crittenden was blamed for the debacle; some critics insisted that his notorious intemperance had caused his failure. Although not found guilty of any charge, his military usefulness was ended. Crittenden resigned his commission in Oc-

27

tober 1862 and spent the rest of the war in various minor positions.

Thomas longed to move into eastern Tennessee, now almost unprotected; but, as he wrote Buell on January 23, the poor roads and inadequate supplies in that area would not support his army. Instead, Buell authorized him to shift to Lebanon, from which point Thomas could cooperate in Buell's impending move toward Bowling Green. On the Confederate side communications were so poor that General Johnston did not learn of the collapse of his right wing until he read an account of the battle in a copy of the Louisville *Democrat* that had reached Bowling Green. If the report was true, he wrote the Richmond authorities, "East Tennessee is wide open to invasion, or, if the plan of the enemy be a combined movement upon Nashville, it is in jeopardy, unless a force can be placed to oppose a movement from Burkesville. . . ." [13]

East Tennessee was one of the least of Johnston's worries, for his line was crumbling at more important points. A small engagement at Belmont, Missouri, on November 7 had convinced General Polk in western Kentucky that he was about to be attacked by a much larger force based on Cairo, Illinois, and Mayfield. The bishop developed a fortress complex and shielded himself at Columbus like a turtle withdrawing into his shell. Polk disclaimed any responsibility for Forts Henry and Donelson, which were supposed to block the Tennessee and Cumberland rivers, and Johnston, preoccupied with his immediate front, never ordered Polk to take the measures that might have saved the western end of the Confederate line in Kentucky.

Both forts were poorly sited, constructed, and manned. Overshadowed by nearby hills, Fort Henry would be flooded during normal winter high water. The artillery here was so placed that it could fire only downstream, and its range was limited. When Johnston assumed his command in September, Fort Donelson had actually been abandoned, for most Tennessee authorities were convinced that the Mississippi River would be the line for a Federal advance in the west. General Lloyd Tilghman of Paducah was appalled by the condition of the forts when he was placed in command of them in November, but he possessed little influence and was unable to secure the improvements that he recommended.

Grant recognized the strategic importance of the Cumberland and Tennessee rivers, and at the end of January 1862 he received permission from General Henry Halleck to move against the forts with the assistance of gunboats. Since Tilghman had fewer than 3,000 men at Fort Henry when the first Union troops appeared on February 5, he wisely evacuated most of his troops before attempting a gallant but futile defense. Andrew H. Foote's gunboats and the rising waters soon rendered the Confederate batteries ineffective, and Tilghman surrendered himself and fewer than 100 men early in the afternoon of February 6. Most of Grant's army had still not arrived, and the victory was a source of deep pride for the freshwater Union navy.

In a belated outburst of activity Johnston ordered Generals Pillow, Buckner, and John B. Floyd to rush to Donelson and help save it. Uncertain even of the number and disposition of his own forces in that area, Johnston abdicated authority by writing Floyd on February 8, "I cannot give you specific instructions and place under your command the entire force." [14]

The Union troops moved slowly and did not arrive before Fort Donelson until February 13. Poorly planned and still incomplete, it had been sited to guard the river and was highly vulnerable to a land attack. Confederate morale was bad, for many of the soldiers realized the predicament in which they had been placed. Supplies were scanty, and sleet and snow accompanied temperatures well below freezing.

Grant's advance units that arrived at Donelson on

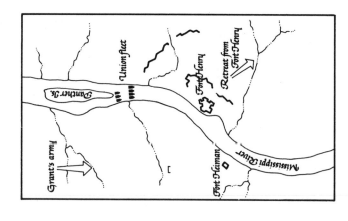

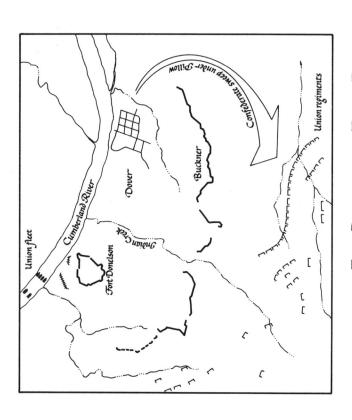

THE CAMPAIGN OF FORTS DONELSON AND HENRY

February 13 numbered only some 12,000 men, while the Confederates had about 15,000. Floyd could have used this temporary superiority either to evacuate the fort safely or to destroy the Union vanguard before it was reinforced. But he vacillated and did neither, and by the next day he was outnumbered, with the odds lengthening steadily. Confederate spirits rose, however, when their river batteries damaged the *Carondelet* as that vessel tried to silence the Confederate guns. The next afternoon five gunboats renewed the attack, but four were disabled in a furious gun battle, and Grant had to revise his plans of capturing Donelson.

As Grant strengthened his infantry positions, Floyd made a belated effort to escape. At cold dawn on February 15 the Confederates attacked, and by noon an escape route to Nashville was almost clear. But no overall plan had been formulated, no one person was in firm control, and the Confederate command again failed when swift action was essential. The Confederate generals engaged in a bitter wrangle at the Dover Inn headquarters that evening about responsibility for the day's debacle and about the next day's course of action. Ignoring Forrest's report that Wynn's Ferry Road was still open, they decided to surrender. Floyd seized the *General Anderson*, the only available steamboat, and fled with his two Virginia regiments. Pillow and the engineer Jeremy Gilmer, who had done all too little to prepare an adequate defense, departed in a rowboat. A raging Forrest refused to surrender and led his troopers through the floodwater to safety, a few infantrymen riding double with them.

Buckner, unhappily left in sole command, proposed to Grant on the morning of February 16 that an armistice halt firing until noon while commissioners agreed upon terms of capitulation. Grant's reply made him an immediate hero in the Union: "No terms except an unconditional and immediate surrender can be accepted. I propose to move immediately upon your works." Grant and

Buckner had been friends at West Point, and in 1854, after Grant's resignation from the army, Buckner had rescued him from an embarrassing financial situation in New York. Buckner may have expected more consideration from his friend, but he had no choice but to "accept the ungenerous and unchivalrous terms which you propose." The surrender involved nearly 12,000 men, 20,000 stands of arms, and 48 artillery pieces. Then Grant took Buckner aside and quietly offered to place at his disposal any money that he needed.[15]

Columbus could no longer be defended, and that powerful bastion was soon evacuated by the Confederates. While the western end of his Kentucky line was disintegrating, Johnston remained preoccupied with the anticipated advance of Buell's army from its bases near Munfordville and South Carrollton on the Green River. Constant rumors reported Union movements, but Johnston was frustrated by his inability to get reliable information. When word arrived of the defeat at Mill Springs and of Grant's advance toward the river forts, Johnston admitted that the Bowling Green defenses on which so much labor had been lavished could not be held. Evacuation of the Confederate capital of Kentucky began on February 11. The two bridges spanning the Barren River were destroyed to impede the Union advance, and fires that broke out during and just after the Confederates' departure heavily damaged the business section of town. Johnston's army retreated to Nashville and then abandoned that city without a struggle. By mid-February 1862 Kentucky was almost cleared of Confederate troops. On March 1 Bowling Green received the first regular United States mail since the arrival of the Confederates the previous September.[16]

3

THE GREAT INVASION

GENERAL JOHNSTON was severely criticized for his retreat from Kentucky, and when he also abandoned Nashville and its vast accumulation of supplies to the enemy, his removal was angrily demanded by critics across the Confederacy. While Johnston assumed the entire blame for the disasters, Davis refused to remove him; and the general began to concentrate his troops at Corinth, Mississippi, where he was joined by Pierre G. T. Beauregard and Braxton Bragg. Unwilling to retreat farther, Johnston decided to strike Grant's army at Pittsburg Landing before it was reinforced by Buell's army from Nashville. The Confederates achieved a tactical surprise on Sunday, April 6, and made good headway before the Federals rallied. During the afternoon of fierce fighting, General Johnston moved to the front to push the attack personally. Struck by a ball that severed a leg artery, he refused to halt for medical aid and bled to death in the saddle, the rebel yell sounding in his ears as his troops fought on around him. Several Kentucky regiments fought on both sides, and Johnston was only one of many Kentuckians who died on that bloody battlefield.

Another casualty on the second day of battle was George Johnson, governor of Confederate Kentucky. He and his associates had accompanied the army on its retreat across Tennessee. Johnson served as a volunteer aide on Breckinridge's staff on Sunday, but, although his horse was killed under him, he wanted more direct participation. Sworn in as a private in Company E, Fourth Kentucky Infantry, he was critically wounded Monday afternoon and left unattended on the field as the Confederate army was pushed back. Finally recognized by Union General Alexander McCook, who had met him at the Charleston Democratic convention in 1860, Johnson was given the best medical care possible. But the doctors could only alleviate his pain, and Governor Johnson died on April 9, many miles from the Kentucky fields he loved. The Provisional Council elected Richard Hawes, a prominent lawyer and politician from Paris, to fill the vacancy.

During the next several months Kentucky was the scene only of minor skirmishes as small Confederate detachments slipped into the state to recruit men and horses, to harass the Union forces, and to hold them away from the major theaters of fighting. Perhaps the most important action was General George W. Morgan's flanking movement that forced the Confederates out of Cumberland Gap in June. Some of the Kentucky fighting consisted of guerrilla action, for which the Confederates were usually blamed. On May 27, 1862, Brigadier General Jeremiah Tilford Boyle, a native of Mercer County, was assigned command of what was later called the District of Kentucky. Determined to halt guerrilla activities and to suppress Confederate support, Boyle violated civil rights and aroused intense opposition to his numerous regulations. Property owners with Confederate sympathies were especially alarmed by the order of June 1 that set the tone for his command: "When damage shall be done to the person or property of *loyal* citizens by marauding bands of guerrillas, the disloyal of the neighborhood will *be held responsible, and a military commission appointed to assess damages and enforce compensation.*" [1]

Those persons accused of aiding the rebellion or sympathizing with it were required to subscribe to a loyalty oath as a condition for release. "I do solemnly swear that I will bear true allegiance to the United States, and support and sustain the Constitution and laws thereof; that I will maintain the national sovereignty paramount to that of all state, county, or Confederate powers; that I will discountenance, discourage, and forever oppose secession, rebellion, and disintegration of the Federal Union; that I disclaim and denounce all faith and fellowship with the so-called Confederate armies; and pledge my honor, my property, and my life to the sacred performance of this my solemn oath of allegiance to the government of the United States of America." [2]

After the battle of Shiloh, Buell's army began a slow advance toward Chattanooga, and the war receded from Kentucky. But General Kirby Smith in eastern Tennessee became increasingly restive with the defensive posture into which he had been thrust. By early July he had indicated to various persons his desire to drive George Morgan from Cumberland Gap, or to invade Middle Tennessee behind Buell, or to move into Kentucky and recover that state for the Confederacy. His desire to invade Kentucky was whetted by the acclaim John Hunt Morgan received for the first of his Kentucky raids.

Although born in Alabama, John Hunt Morgan had strong Kentucky ties, and he was educated at Lexington's Transylvania College. After Mexican War service Morgan manufactured hemp products and conducted a general merchandising business in Lexington. He joined the Confederate army at Bowling Green and soon became noted for the hard-riding raids that became his trademark. His dash and audacity delighted many Southerners, who called him the Jeb Stuart of the West. Some orthodox military men, however, questioned the worth of his spectacular exploits, suggesting that he seldom accomplished anything of permanent value. Basil Duke, Morgan's second in command and brother-in-law, and George St. Leger Grenfell, an able if erratic British soldier of fortune, did much to compensate for Morgan's recklessness and disdain for such details as discipline. After the retreat from Kentucky, Morgan and his men had been active in Tennessee, clashing repeatedly with Colonel Frank Wolford and his "wild riders" of the First Kentucky Union Cavalry.

Morgan and his men longed to return home, and in May 1862 he led some 50 men across the border with the avowed aim of disrupting the Union line of communication. They took a look at Glasgow but decided to bypass it when they learned that a 500-man garrison was stationed there. They had better luck at Cave City, where they captured two trains. One was destroyed, but the other carried a number of Federal officers and their wives, and after the chagrined men had been paroled, Morgan gallantly returned the train for their trip back to Louisville. The raid actually accomplished little except to agitate some Union officials, but it encouraged Morgan to undertake another expedition, and its success made it easier for him to secure permission to stage a larger enterprise.

Successful recruiting in Kentucky and the return from Virginia of 200 Kentuckians who had served there in the First Kentucky Infantry enabled Morgan to build up his Second Kentucky Cavalry. Grenfell provided invaluable assistance in training the new men, and they developed a respectful affection for their mad Englishman. But he was never able to instill the discipline he had learned in the British army. "I never encountered such men," he complained, "who would fight like the devil, but would do as they pleased, like these damned Rebel cavalrymen." [3]

On the Fourth of July, 1862, Morgan led 876 officers and men westward from Knoxville in his first major Kentucky raid. Turning north at Sparta, they entered Kentucky after a night crossing of the Cumberland and captured Tompkinsville on July 9 in a brief fire fight that

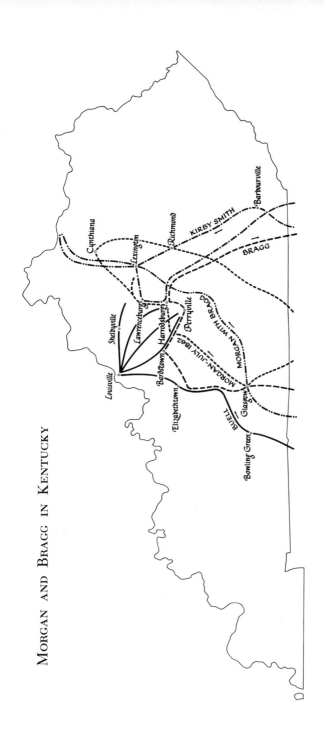

MORGAN AND BRAGG IN KENTUCKY

Barbourville

KIRBY SMITH

Richmond

BRAGG

Cynthiana

Lexington

Shelbyville

Lawrenceburg

Harrodsburg

Perryville

MORGAN WITH BRAGG

Louisville

Bardstown

MORGAN—JULY 1862

Elizabethtown

BUELL

Glasgow

Bowling Green

netted them 300 prisoners. Then they rode to Glasgow, the home of most of the men in Company C. A heavy thunderstorm pelted the column as it neared Horse Cave, and the men sought shelter, while Morgan and a few companions rode on ahead. Among them was George Ellsworth, the telegrapher genius, whose work during the violent storm earned for him the name "Lightning."

The Confederates forded the Green River and took Lebanon on July 12, capturing 200 of the enemy and a large depot of supplies. Much of Kentucky was panic-stricken by this time. Morgan's command was expanded into a sizable army, and it was reliably reported to be in several parts of the state at the same time. After receiving frantic appeals for help, Lincoln sent word to Halleck: "They are having a stampede in Kentucky. Please look to it." General Boyle sought command assistance from General Nelson, who was then in Nashville: "I have no officers fit for the field. . . . Can you come?" His plea was reinforced by one from John W. Fennell, adjutant of the Kentucky Volunteers, who wired: "They are playing Hell in all the Central Counties. Are beating our forces in detail. We have no one in the field worth a damn." [4]

After a Sunday picnic in Harrodsburg, Confederate detachments trotted off to cut Bluegrass railroads while the main body moved toward Lexington. But that city was strongly held, and Morgan's troopers spent the night at nearby Georgetown. Several Confederates slipped across the Union lines to enjoy brief and dangerous visits with families and friends, and a few volunteers managed to get through to join Morgan's command. Despite the stirring rhetoric of his recruiting proclamation—"I come to liberate you from the despotism of a tyrannical faction and to rescue my native State from the hand of your oppressors"—Morgan was not overwhelmed by the number of volunteers.[5]

Cynthiana was stoutly defended by a motley but determined group that included the Eighteenth Kentucky Infantry and some Cincinnati firemen, but after two hours the surviving Federals surrendered or fled. Since Morgan's pursuers were gaining on him, the prisoners were quickly paroled and the weary Confederates pushed on through Paris. At Richmond they acquired 50 welcome recruits. Although Federal units were reported on every side, Morgan managed to elude them as he picked his way southward. During the brief halt at Somerset, Ellsworth sent infuriating telegrams to several of the Confederates' particular enemies, including the editor George Prentice and General Boyle. The message to the latter, carrying Morgan's name, said: "Good Morning, Jerry. The telegraph is a great institution. You should destroy it as it keeps me posted too well. My friend Ellsworth has all your dispatches since July 10 on file. Do you want copies?" [6]

In seeking permission for even larger raids, Morgan boasted that he had captured and paroled 1,200 enemy soldiers, recruited 300 men, "secured" several hundred horses, and used or destroyed extensive supplies in seventeen towns. His casualties totaled fewer than 100 men. The consternation spread by his appearance restricted thousands of Union soldiers to guard duty in an effort to protect vital railroads, bridges, and supply depots. Union General Jacob D. Cox resorted to poetry in an effort to discredit Morgan's acquisition of mounts.

> *John Morgan's foot is on thy shore*
> *Kentucky! O Kentucky!*
> *His hand is on thy stable door*
> *Kentucky! O Kentucky!*
> *You'll see your good gray mare no more,*
> *He'll ride her till her back is sore*
> *And leave her at some stranger's door,*
> *Kentucky! O Kentucky!* [7]

Morgan's reports of his exploits increased Kirby Smith's determination to invade Kentucky with his army. An obvious complication was the need to coordinate his moves with those of General Bragg, whose aim was to smash Buell's army in Middle Tennessee before undertaking any other scheme. The Confederate government had not provided a clear delineation of power between the generals, and a persistent Smith was able to impose his will on Bragg. Smith was aided by the insistence of many exiled Kentuckians who swore that the commonwealth had been kept in the Union against the wishes of a majority of her citizens. Given an opportunity, they declared, Kentucky would turn against her oppressors, and the boundary of the Confederacy would leap northward to the Ohio River. During the summer Bragg moved his army to Chattanooga, and Morgan and Forrest slashed at Buell's supply lines until he had to suspend his slow advance toward that city. By early August the Confederates were ready to take the offensive.

Bragg and Smith conferred at Chattanooga on July 31. Bragg did not assert his seniority, and they apparently agreed to operate independently until they should come together in Kentucky, when Bragg would assume overall command. This decision insured that the campaign would be poorly coordinated, for Smith did not like to serve under anyone, and he would not relinquish his independent command if he could avoid doing so. The plans made at the conference were vague, complex, and subject to various interpretations. Smith would force Federal General George W. Morgan out of Cumberland Gap. Then he would either participate in a move against Buell in Middle Tennessee or advance into Kentucky. General Humphrey Marshall, a massively proportioned Kentucky lawyer and politician who commanded 3,000 men in western Virginia, was to seal off the northern exit from Cumberland Gap when Smith moved against its defenders. John C. Breckinridge, then leading a division in Earl Van Dorn's army, was invited to join the impending festivities; his presence in Kentucky was expected to attract substantial support. In an unusually jocular mood Bragg wrote Brickinridge on August 8: "My army has promised to make me military governor of Ohio in ninety days. . . , and as they can not do this without passing your home, I have thought you would like to have an escort to visit your family." [8] Other Confederate armies in the West were expected to cooperate by exerting enough pressure to keep reinforcements from going to Buell.

Smith's army marched on the night of August 13. Moving swiftly through the Cumberland Mountains, they took Barbourville on August 18 and snapped up 50 wagons carrying provisions to the Gap. Determined to proceed on his own independent course, Smith informed his superiors that the lack of supplies in a generally hostile area left him no alternative but to advance toward Lexington; he would not be able to join Bragg for an attack on Buell in the Nashville area.

When Smith learned that heavy Union reinforcements were expected at Richmond, he decided to attack before they arrived. The battle opened early on the morning of August 30 at Kingston, a small village south of Richmond. By midafternoon the stubborn Union troops had been pushed back to a ridge south of the larger town. General Nelson had not intended to fight there, because his inexperienced troops needed more training; but his orders to retreat on Lexington were not delivered to a senior officer until after the engagement was under way. Late in the afternoon the weary, thirsty Confederates made one supreme effort, and the Union line cracked at each end. Nelson propelled his vast bulk along the front in a vain effort to steady and inspire his inexperienced troops. "If they can't hit me they can't hit anything!" he assured them. But he was soon struck twice, and sudden panic swept through the ranks.[9]

As the Union soldiers fled northward, John Scott's

cavalry slashed in to cut off their retreat. Nelson was captured but then managed to escape in the confusion of the battlefield. He left behind 1,000 casualties and 4,300 prisoners from his army of some 6,500 men. The Confederates occupied Lexington on September 1 and Frankfort two days later. The Union line was suddenly back on the Ohio, and such river ports as Louisville, Cincinnati, Newport, and Covington were panic-stricken. Many civilians and some troops fled across the river; others worked frantically to construct defenses that might save their towns. A visitor to Louisville found "the city in great confusion, all the stores . . . closed and troops . . . dashing about at a great rate," while the hotels were crowded with refugees.[10] The editor of the Louisville *Weekly Journal* exhorted his readers on September 16: "We have time enough for everything but inactivity."

But Smith did not use the advantage he had created. He relinquished the initiative, scattered his troops over much of the Bluegrass, and waited passively for something to happen. During most of this period he was out of touch with Bragg despite the obvious need for a coordinated campaign. Bragg had waited for his supply train to catch up with him and had not left Chattanooga until August 28. He had at last abandoned his hope of defeating Buell in Middle Tennessee before moving into Kentucky. Now, he wrote Breckinridge, he would elude the Federal army and march into central Kentucky, where he hoped to find Smith. But his plans were still vague as his grey columns trudged northward across Tennessee; his lack of knowledge of Smith's position and intentions made it difficult for Bragg to formulate a campaign strategy.

Misled by false reports of ample supplies in the Glasgow area, Bragg swung west of the line of march he had first selected. He was appalled when Forrest reported on September 9 that at least half of Buell's army was north of Nashville and marching toward the strong fortifications at Bowling Green. Buell had been uncertain of the Confederates' intentions, but he had concentrated his army at Nashville since that important supply point seemed their most likely target. Grant forwarded several thousand reinforcements, and when Bragg was reliably reported crossing into Kentucky, Buell's confidence soared. "I believe Nashville can be held and Kentucky rescued," he wired Halleck. "What I have will be sufficient here with the defenses that are being prepared, and I propose to move with the remainder of the army against the enemy in Kentucky." [11]

Leaving General Thomas to guard the city, Buell marched for Bowling Green, whose strong fortifications stood only about thirty miles west of Glasgow. Deciding en route that Nashville was no longer seriously threatened, Buell ordered Thomas to join him with two additional divisions.

Once Bragg had decided to avoid a clash with Buell in Tennessee, he should have made every effort to achieve his goals in Kentucky, including a concentration with Smith, before Buell could arrive. But after an excellent start Bragg delayed three days at Sparta, Tennessee, and on September 14, when he reached Glasgow, Buell's army was already entering Bowling Green. The need for speed was urgent, but Bragg became embroiled in an unusual affair at Munfordville, where he won a battle that helped lose a campaign.

The vital Louisville and Nashville Railroad crossed the Green River at Munfordville on five massive spans that towered 115 feet above the river and attracted Confederate raiders as a candle attracts moths. In mid-September 1862 the position was guarded by a detachment commanded by Colonel John T. Wilder, a thirty-two-year-old iron manufacturer from Indiana. After his arrival on September 8 Wilder drove his men hard to strengthen the inadequate defenses, but much still needed to be done when, on Saturday evening, September 13, he received a demand to surrender from Colonel John Scott, who had been sent by Kirby Smith to locate Bragg. Wilder refused, and Scott sought the aid of General James R. Chalmers and his Mississippi brigade, who were at nearby Cave City. Acting on his own initiative, Chalmers moved up to support Scott, and the Confederates attacked at early dawn on Sunday morning. The Union troops repulsed them with murderous rifle fire that inflicted more than 200 casualties.

At midmorning Chalmers penned another demand for surrender "to avoid further bloodshed." Wilder replied tartly: "If you want to avoid further bloodshed keep out of the range of my guns." [12] The arrival of reinforcements, though complicating the command situation because Colonel Cyrus L. Dunham was senior to Wilder, brought the strength of the Federal garrison to 4,000 men. Chalmers and Scott, conceding that the nut was too hard for them to crack, sought assistance from the main army at Glasgow.

Bragg was furious when he learned of Chalmers's "unauthorized and unjudicious" action, but he agreed that the Union position would now have to be taken. The army started moving out of Glasgow on September 15, and on the next day a fuming Bragg arrived at Munfordville to take personal charge of the unfortunate affair. General Buckner, whose home was nearby, persuaded his irate superior to surround the Union force instead of launching a massive assault that might endanger the town and its inhabitants. General William J. Hardee positioned his troops on the south side of the river, while General Polk crossed upstream from the Union fortifications and moved in behind the defenders. These dispositions took time, and Bragg delayed the final assault until Wednesday morning, September 17. Wilder's weary men continued to beat off minor probing attacks.

Late Tuesday afternoon Bragg again demanded capitulation to avoid "the terrible consequences of assault." A council of war called by Colonel Dunham concluded that resistance was impossible if the Confederates really had the overwhelming force they claimed. Dunham telegraphed this decision to Louisville, and he was ordered to turn his command over to Wilder; when Dunham refused to serve under an officer junior in rank, he was ordered to place himself under arrest. Wilder agreed with his predecessor that surrender should be considered if the situation was really hopeless. But he was not a professional soldier, and he was uncertain about the honorable course of action to follow under such conditions as he faced. Should he accept or reject Bragg's ultimatum to surrender unconditionally within an hour? In his dilemma the Hoosier officer paid Buckner a supreme compliment.

When Wilder and Buckner met under another flag of truce late Tuesday evening, Wilder astounded the Kentuckian by declaring, "I came to you to find out what I ought to do." Military matters were not usually handled that way, Buckner protested, but the approach intrigued him. "I wouldn't have deceived that man under those circumstances for anything," he later explained.[13] When Buckner repeated that the Federals were trapped by a much larger army that would overrun them at dawn, Wilder replied that his troops "had been summoned four times to surrender, with like assurances of their power to compel it, and we at each time successfully repelled the attack. . . ." Could he see for himself if he was now hopelessly outnumbered?

Buckner did not hesitate; he was so delighted by the affair that Wilder's request seemed quite logical. Colonel Wilder was escorted around the southern portion of the Confederate lines while his adjutant checked the forces north of the river. When they compared counts, Wilder concluded that Buckner had not exaggerated. "Well, it seems to me, General Buckner, that I ought to surrender." But Buckner had become so thoroughly enmeshed in his role that he cautioned Wilder to wait: "If you have information that would induce you to think, that the sacrificing of every man at this place would give your army an advantage elsewhere, it is your duty to do it." Wilder considered the situation carefully, but he had no such information. "I believe that I will surrender," he said.[14]

Details were arranged during the early morning hours, and at six o'clock on September 17 the Union troops marched to nearby Rowlett's Station, the surrender point. The 155 officers and 3,921 men were immediately paroled, provided with rations, and directed toward Bowling Green, where their presence might complicate Buell's supply problem. In General Orders, Bragg congratulated his army on its victory but warned: "Our labors are not over. A powerful foe is assembling in our front and we must prepare to strike him a sudden and decisive blow. A short time can therefore be given for repose, when we must resume our march to still more brilliant victories." The following day was to be devoted to such repose and to thanksgiving and prayer.[15]

Bragg may have sought divine guidance himself, for he was still uncertain of his next move. On the evening of Wilder's surrender he learned that Buell's army was already on the road north of Bowling Green, but the reports failed to reveal clearly the intentions of the Union army. Buckner's division was moved southward, either as a reconnaissance in force or as a possible attempt to lure Buell into attacking, but no serious contact was made. Bragg wavered for another day while the Union army flowed up to and by him to the west; then on September 20 the well-rested Confederates at last resumed their march northward. At Nolin, Bragg turned his column toward Bardstown, where Kirby Smith was expected to join him. But Smith was not there, and Bragg abandoned his hope of capturing Louisville and went on the defensive. Buell arrived in Louisville on September 25 and in a commendable outburst of energy set to work immediately to prepare his army for an advance against the enemy, who occupied most of the Bluegrass and spilled out over its edges.

Despondent over his failure to attain a major goal, Bragg began to consider retiring to Danville or some other suitable point where he could concentrate his scattered troops and perhaps fight upon ground of his choosing. As early as September 25 he warned General Samuel Cooper, Confederate adjutant and inspector general, that Kentucky might have to be abandoned with the possibility of heavy losses as the Confederate army retreated.[16] Bragg was beginning to realize that he had not required the concerted effort necessary to make his strategy work. His most serious blunder had been—and continued to be—the failure to achieve close coordination with Smith. The fault was certainly not all Bragg's; Smith had shown only a remote interest in what Bragg was doing; but the final responsibility belonged to Braxton Bragg.

Instead of joining Bragg at Bardstown, Smith had actually moved away from that point. He had assumed that Humphrey Marshall would be able to cut off George Morgan if the latter attempted to escape from his precarious position at Cumberland Gap. Marshall got into position at Mount Sterling to intercept Morgan, and Smith rushed troops there to insure the kill. But George Morgan escaped the trap, fought off John Hunt Morgan, who tried to check him, and made a brilliant forced march to the safety of the Ohio River. As a consequence of this affair, the Confederate troops in Kentucky were more widely dispersed than ever.

But on one important point the Confederate commanders were united: they shared a bitter disappointment over the failure of Kentuckians to join their armies in large numbers. The wagon trains had hauled thousands of stands of arms to equip the anticipated horde of volunteers, but most of the rifles remained in the wagons, despite the obvious Confederate sympathy of many of the state's inhabitants. "Their hearts were evidently with us, but their blue-grass and fat-grass [cattle] are against us," Smith complained to Bragg.[17] Recruitment might have been more successful had the immensely popular Breckinridge been there as a rallying point, but he was delayed so long in leaving Van Dorn's command that the invasion had ended before he could get to Kentucky. Bragg and Smith sought recruits to help insure victory; many Confederate sympathizers demanded a victory first.

Once he assumed the defensive, Bragg's plan was to defeat the Union army on a field of his own choosing, and then seek the important objectives, such as Louisville and Cincinnati, that had eluded his grasp. Since his army could not be concentrated indefinitely at one spot, Bragg dispersed his troops over a wide area, with Polk near Bardstown, Pat Cleburne and Preston Smith at Shelbyville, Harry Heth at Georgetown, and Carter Stevenson near Danville. Kirby Smith, near Frankfort, was still operating independently. The order of concentration would have to depend upon Buell's line of approach, but it would have to be done quickly or the Confederates might be destroyed piecemeal by the much larger Union army.

Bragg himself paid a visit to Frankfort. There was some forlorn hope that the establishment here of the Confederate government of Kentucky would spur enlistments. It would create an aura of permanence that the government in exile had not been able to present; indeed, it could even provide for conscription, which often had a salutary effect upon volunteering. Governor Hawes had been in Virginia when the invasion started, but he passed through Chattanooga on September 17 and caught up with the army a few days later. On October 3 Bragg wrote Polk from Frankfort: "Tomorrow we inaugurate the civil Governor here, and transfer to him all that department." [18]

The ceremonies began at noon before a large audience of soldiers and civilians. Relying on Bragg's promises, Hawes assured his listeners that his government would remain in Frankfort and that the commonwealth would soon be free of enemy troops. But Union General Joshua Sill was already nearing the city, and by midafternoon the Confederates were hastily evacuating the capital. Governor Hawes left the executive mansion he had occupied for a few hours, and the great inaugural ball planned for that evening was never held. For the rest of the war the Confederate government of Kentucky was in exile, sometimes with the western armies, in which so many Kentuckians fought, and sometimes in Richmond, where it survived on the charity of the Confederate States of America. The council passed laws and the governor issued orders, but they had no appreciable effect on the course of events in Kentucky.

Bragg had grossly underestimated Buell's ability to prepare rapidly for an advance. The Confederate general had anticipated a respite of several weeks, but even as he prepared for Hawes's inauguration, a large force of Union cavalry was reported near Shelbyville. Then Shelbyville was reported captured as Cleburne pulled back rapidly to avoid being overrun. Frankfort was suddenly endangered, and Bragg's army faced the prospects of being sliced in half. He issued vague orders for Frankfort to be held while Polk smashed into the flank of the Union army. But Polk was also under heavy pressure at Bardstown and was pulling back his advance units to save them; it was doubtful that he could hold his position, much less make the flank attack. After meeting with his subordinates, Polk began withdrawing toward the army's depot at Bryantsville. His report to Bragg was vague and incomplete at a time when the commanding general needed all possible assistance in arriving at some decision that might retrieve the deteriorating situation.

The confused and underinformed Confederate commander decided to retreat to Harrodsburg, where Polk would join him. But Kirby Smith asked for and received permission to remain north of the Kentucky River; he thought that he might be able to hold Lexington against what he assumed was Buell's main thrust. Although Bragg lacked information about both the enemy and his own forces, he wrote Smith on October 5: "It is my intention to move on the enemy whether at Shelbyville or Frankfort as soon as my force arrives here." [19] Since Polk had not indicated strong pressure on his front, Bragg assumed that Smith was correct in believing that the main Union advance was against him. Bragg began to plan a move to Versailles, west of Lexington, where he could cooperate with Smith to halt Buell's army. But Buell's advance resembled a giant hand thrust southeastward from Louisville, and only one finger was directed toward Kirby Smith's position; the major confrontation would occur elsewhere.

On the night of October 6 General Hardee camped his troops around Perryville, where water was available in Salt River and some smaller streams (a prolonged drought had severely complicated the problem of finding adequate supplies of water for large bodies of men and horses). The next day Joe Wheeler's hard-working cavalrymen reported Union infantry in the vicinity. Hardee was not alarmed, although he did forward the report to Polk. In midafternoon Hardee wrote Bragg that Wheeler was being pushed hard and a fight would probably occur the next day. If Bragg was not occupied elsewhere, perhaps he might send some reinforcements and come to assume personal command. Hardee's words still carried no sense of urgency despite his postbattle claims that he had provided ample warning and had advised Bragg to concentrate the entire Confederate army at Perryville.

Annoyed by the threat against Perryville, Bragg ordered Polk to send Ben Cheatham's division back to help Hardee rout the enemy before coming on to Versailles. The Federal forces nearing Perryville had increased ominously by October 8, and Polk hastily summoned a council of war that morning to decide what should be done. Bragg had ordered an immediate attack on what he thought was a relatively minor force, but the council's decision was to take a defensive position on a ridge east of Chaplin's Fork, a small stream on the west side of Perryville. Yet when Polk wrote Bragg, he did not indicate that he was outnumbered, he did not request reinforcements, and he did not report the council's decision to go on the defensive. Bragg made many mistakes of his own during the Kentucky campaign, but blame for his failure to concentrate his forces for the decisive battle in Kentucky must be accorded in large measure to Smith, Polk, and Hardee, who failed to supply him with the information needed for a competent decision. Few Confederate armies ever experienced such a disastrous breakdown of communications among senior officers.

Bragg rode to Perryville on October 8 to brush off the mysterious enemy force that was disrupting his plans. Angered by the defensive stance Polk had assumed, Bragg began shifting his troops for an assault that he hoped to launch about one o'clock that afternoon. Polk would open the affair on the right by sending Cheatham's division against the Yankees who occupied a ridge west of shallow Doctor's Fork. Then Hardee would advance the center and left of the Confederate line, and the troublesome Federals would be crushed.

The difficulty was that Buell had been informed that Bragg's main army was at Perryville and he was concentrating the bulk of his command, some 58,000 men, at that point. Sill, with 12,000 men on the left of the Union advance, was occupying Kirby Smith's attention. Charles C. Gilbert's corps was in the center of the forces approaching Perryville, with McCook on the left and Thomas L. Crittenden on the right. General George H. Thomas, Buell's second in command, accompanied Crittenden. The flanks were supposed to be on a line with Gilbert and ready to attack by early morning, October 8.

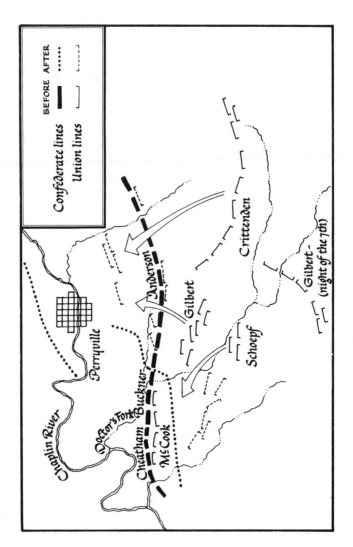

THE BATTLE OF PERRYVILLE

Both were late, and the morning's activities consisted largely of minor skirmishing, some desultory exchanges of artillery fire, and a futile Confederate effort to drive the Federals away from the precious pools of water in Doctor's Fork. Troops in both armies suffered from thirst as the day wore on.

The Confederate attack was delayed by the appearance of a Union column that could have struck Polk's flank had he exposed it, but finally Cheatham moved toward his objective. Well-sited Union artillery caused heavy casualties in his division and forced the survivors to seek shelter in a patch of trees. George Maney's Tennessee brigade followed in support, was checked, then surged forward under his leadership and broke the Union line. Much of McCook's corps was thrown into disorder, but some seasoned troops fought desperately and slowed the Confederate advance. Shoved back nearly three-quarters of a mile, McCook asked General Phil Sheridan of Gilbert's corps for help, but Sheridan was engaged with two Confederate brigades and could not give assistance.

Atmospheric quirks apparently prevented both Bragg and Buell from hearing the early battle sounds. When the thunder of the guns and the crackle of rifle fire finally reached Buell after three o'clock, he sent General Gilbert to find out what was happening. As news arrived, Buell finally realized that a major engagement was well under way and that matters were not going well for him. When darkness fell over the parched battlefield, his right wing had been badly mauled and his army had suffered casualties of 845 killed, 2,851 wounded, and 515 missing. Confederate losses had also been heavy: 510 killed, 2,635 wounded, and 251 missing. In his official report Bragg asserted, "For the time engaged, it was the severest and most desperately contested engagement within my knowledge." [20]

While details sought the wounded, and thirsty soldiers searched for water, Bragg, Polk, and Hardee assessed their situation. Although they had gained the day's advantage, their losses had been extremely heavy in proportion to the number engaged. With 15,000 men they had fought most of the Army of the Ohio. Their weak left flank had endured severe pressure; a Union brigade had actually penetrated Perryville before being expelled. The weary, outnumbered Confederates might be overwhelmed when fighting resumed at dawn. Retreat was the only way to save what remained of the army, and on October 9 Bragg pulled back to Harrodsburg, where he hoped to unite all his forces. But Harrodsburg was also a potential trap, with the Federals threatening to envelop it; and Bragg continued his retreat toward Bryantsville, his main supply depot. The busy Wheeler reported Yankee efforts to outflank the Confederate army and cut it off from Cumberland Gap.

At last aware of their danger, the Confederates began to join forces. Smith reached Harrodsburg on October 10 as Polk led his men across Dick's River toward Bryantsville. The close pursuit by strong Union units forced Bragg to form a battle line along Salt River with Smith's troops and the tail end of Polk's column. Wheeler fought savagely to hold Danville as long as possible, and Humphrey Marshall struggled to control the Kentucky River bridge on the Cumberland Gap road.

On October 12 Bragg assembled Smith, Polk, Cheatham, Hardee, and Marshall for a council of war to discuss future plans. Finally convinced that his great invasion had failed, Bragg concluded that he must preserve his army in order to oppose a Union march into the deep South. Sterling Price and Van Dorn had been crushed at Corinth on October 3-4, and only Bragg's army could prevent the capture of Chattanooga and points south. The 2,500 Kentuckians who had joined the Confederate "army of liberation" did not even compensate for the campaign's losses, and they fell far short of the 20,000 to 30,000 volunteers who had been expected to rally to the Stars and Bars. Bragg had declared earlier that the army could not remain in Kentucky unless a large number of Kentuckians joined it. They had not done so, and Bragg commented bitterly to his wife: "Why then should I stay with my handful of brave Southern men to fight for cowards who sulked about in the dark to say to us, 'We are with you, only whip these fellows out of our country, and let us see you can protect us, and we will join you.' " [21] Such sentiments helped make Bragg the most unpopular general of the Confederate army among Kentuckians.

When the Confederate generals decided that retreat was necessary before they were cut off, Marshall was given permission to remain in the Bluegrass as long as possible; then he was to go to western Virginia. The rest of the army began moving at daybreak on October 13 toward Cumberland Gap, the long lines of wagons creaking their way in the van and Wheeler's weary horsemen helping protect the rear. The supply trains still carried the thousands of unissued weapons that were to have armed Kentucky's volunteers.

Buell pursued the Confederates as far as London, but he was unable to force an engagement, as Wheeler conducted a brilliant rearguard action. Buell terminated the chase there and prepared to shift his army back to Nashville, where he would resume his drive into the Southern heartland. His superiors were not pleased with his plans and the escape of the Confederate army. "I am directed by the President," Halleck wrote, "to say to you that your army must enter East Tennessee this fall, and that it ought to move there while the roads are passable. . . . He does not understand why we cannot march as the enemy marches, live as he lives, and fight as he fights, unless we admit the inferiority of our troops and our generals." One of his soldiers complained that Buell "has shown himself to be ether a coward or a Trator, for with such a force as ours, properly handled, old Bragg could never have escaped." [22] Buell was unable to convince his superiors of the soundness of his plan, but he began to shift his army westward anyway. By the time it reached the vicinity of Glasgow and Bowling Green, he was no longer its commander. Replaced by General William S. Rosecrans, the savior of Kentucky went to Indianapolis to wait for orders.

4

THE END OF
THE STRUGGLE

THE 1862 INVASION of Kentucky was the high-water mark of the Confederacy in the West. The state would be the scene of numerous minor actions during the rest of the war; but after Bragg and Kirby Smith led their weary troops into Tennessee, the Confederate threat to seize Kentucky was at an end. During the next two and a half years the most important Confederate incursions were those of John Hunt Morgan, but they were raids designed to destroy bridges and railroads, capture horses and supplies, gain recruits, and disrupt the Union war effort as much as possible by tying down troops that could have been used elsewhere. Such raids were annoying, sometimes even embarrassing, but they did not pose a serious threat to Union forces in the state.

As the Confederate forces withdrew from the state, the Kentuckians felt betrayed by the refusal of their generals to fight a decisive battle. "With the failure to hold Kentucky," Duke later wrote, "our best and last chance to win the war was thrown away. . . . All the subsequent tremendous struggle was but the dying agony of a great cause, and a gallant people." [1] The Kentucky soldiers blamed Bragg more than Smith for the debacle, and much of their scorn for Bragg came from their belief that he lacked the courage to fight.

As the Confederate infantry toiled toward the safety of Cumberland Gap, it became apparent that the Union pursuit did not represent a real threat. Morgan's Second Kentucky Cavalry was helping cover Kirby Smith's retreat, and about October 15 Morgan apparently discussed with Smith the possibility of his swinging back through the Bluegrass, damaging Buell's supply lines, and entering Tennessee somewhere west of Bowling Green. Such a raid would do something to restore morale, and it would allow Morgan and his men to dissociate themselves from the ignominious retreat of the main army. There is some doubt that Smith positively sanctioned the move, but he did not veto the request, and that was good enough for Morgan.

The Second Kentucky turned northward on October 17 and, using backroads to avoid the enemy, reached Lexington on October 18. There they routed the Fourth Ohio Cavalry that was guarding the town, although some Confederate units fired on each other in the confusion of an early dawn attack. Three hundred prisoners were paroled, and almost before sympathizers could unfurl their Confederate flags, Morgan's column was on the road toward Versailles. Pursued by Union General Ebenezer Dumont, who had surprised and embarrassed him at Lebanon, Tennessee, the previous spring, Morgan moved swiftly through Lawrenceburg and Bloomfield. "Hour after hour we rode, men and horses exhausted," one of Morgan's men later recalled. "As soon as one horse gave out another was procured and the ride continued through all that day and all that night. . . . At day-light no signs of the enemy were seen." [2]

On the night of October 19 a patrol led by Lieutenant James Sale of E Company intercepted a Union supply train near Bardstown. Most of the wagons and their contents had to be burned, except for two sutlers' wagons whose loads of boots and gingerbread were rushed back to the main body. Other detachments screened the column's progress and confused the pursuers, and the Confederates passed leisurely through Elizabethtown on October 20. They disrupted traffic on the L & N Railroad, and then rode on to Morgantown, where they crossed the Green River on October 22. An unseasonable snowstorm swirled in when they reached Greenville, and by morning Duke found the field in which his men had camped "marked by white mounds, under each of which lay one or more sleepers. The field really looked like a grave yard enshrouded in snow." [3]

Any danger of being caught had ended, and the cavalrymen frolicked through lovely Indian summer weather that quickly melted the snow to Hopkinsville, where they had many supporters. Morgan lingered there for five days, resting his men and horses and trying unsuccessfully to persuade Colonel Thomas G. Woodward to resolve an unfortunate duplication of unit designations by merging his Second Kentucky Cavalry with Morgan's. On November 1 Morgan crossed the Tennessee line and camped near Springfield. Within a few days he was actively engaged in the same game of raid and counterraid that had enlivened existence in northern Tennessee the previous spring.

In December, Morgan was promoted to the rank of brigadier general, and his command was increased to brigade strength with the Second, Third, Eighth, Ninth, Tenth, and Eleventh Kentucky regiments and the Fourteenth Tennessee. The social event of the season was Morgan's December wedding to Miss Martha Ready of Murfreesboro; General Polk performed the ceremony. Many of Morgan's men later dated the change in their fortunes from the day of the marriage. Morgan's honeymoon was brief, for Bragg had decided to send him back into Kentucky to cut General Rosecrans's L & N supply line. All indications were that Rosecrans planned to initiate a winter campaign as soon as sufficient supplies were accumulated at his Nashville base. The L & N tracks were now heavily guarded, but Morgan decided that the two massive trestles north of Elizabethtown where the line traversed Muldraugh's Hill might be vulnerable. Forrest was sent into western Tennessee on a similar mission, but Bragg's decision to mount the raids came too late to prevent an engagement of the armies at Stone's River at the end of the year.

Organized into the First Brigade under Duke and the Second Brigade under William C. P. Breckinridge, the Confederates started on Morgan's "Christmas Raid" on December 22. They crossed the Kentucky line on Christmas Eve, when Lieutenant James McCreary wrote: "Cheer after cheer and shout after shout echoed for miles toward the rear of the column, breaking the stillness of the night. Tonight we are camped on the sacred soil of old Kentucky and it fills my heart with joy. . . . campfires illuminate every hill and valley and the fires burn brighter, seemingly are more cheerful, because it is the fatherland." [4] Christmas for Morgan's men was also brightened by the capture of a huge twenty-horse sutler's wagon loaded with delicacies for the Union garrison at Glasgow. They camped that night five miles from Glasgow, and some of the scouts who slipped into town encountered Union soldiers as they all converged on a saloon.

The raiders rode through Glasgow on Christmas Day, then headed for Munfordville on the Green River. After fighting a small skirmish at Bear Wallow, they crossed the river in a cold rain. The Union troops guarding the Bacon Creek bridge of the L & N resisted stubbornly before surrendering, but the bridge was destroyed for the third time. Several miles of track were torn up, and Rosecrans's supply line was disrupted, regardless of what might happen later.

As they approached Elizabethtown on December 27, the Confederates were summoned to surrender by Colonel H. S. Smith, the Federal commander, who told them they were surrounded.[5] Morgan insisted that Smith had reversed the actual situation; he was the one who

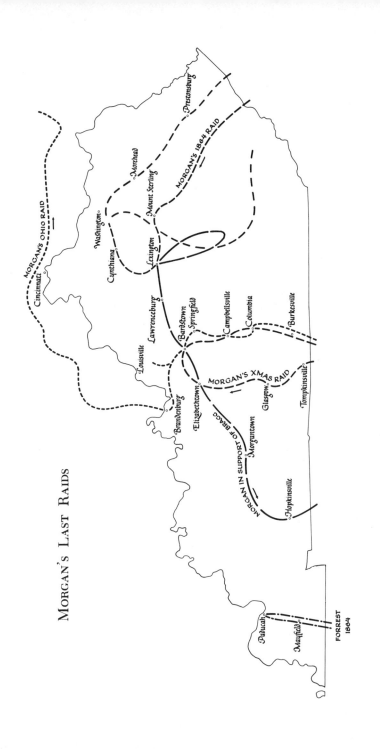

MORGAN'S LAST RAIDS

Prestonburg

MORGAN'S 1864 RAID

Morehead

Washington

Mount Sterling

Cynthiana

Lexington

MORGAN'S OHIO RAID

Cincinnati

Lawrenceburg

Bardstown

Springfield

Campbellsville

Columbia

Burkesville

Louisville

Tompkinsville

Brandenburg

Elizabethtown

MORGAN'S XMAS RAID

Glasgow

Morguntown

MORGAN IN SUPPORT OF BRAGG

Hopkinsville

Paducah

Mayfield

FORREST
1864

should capitulate, since it was he who was surrounded. Smith fought briskly for a short while, and then ran up the white flag for his 600 men. The next day the Confederates captured the stockades that guarded the railroad trestles and burned the massive structures. It was March 1863 before service was restored on that portion of the L & N. His mission accomplished, Morgan turned his attention to the problem of escaping to Tennessee through the net of Union troops bent on destroying him. His decision was to move eastward before turning south; a visit to his beloved Bluegrass was a lure he could seldom resist.

Colonel John M. Harlan was so close that his artillery shelled Morgan's rearguard as it crossed the flooded Rolling Fork River on December 29. Duke, struck by a shell fragment, was loaded into a carriage and hurried to Bardstown for medical attention. General Boyle heard that Duke had been killed and sent Lincoln a gleeful report to that effect. But Duke responded to medical attention, and when the Confederates left Bardstown the next day, the commander of the First Brigade accompanied them, lolling in unusual comfort in a buggy cushioned with featherbeds.

A freezing rain plagued the camp at Springfield, and Tom Quirk's scouts said that several thousand aroused Federals were concentrated at Lebanon, only nine miles away. Ten thousand others were reported blocking the roads to the Cumberland River; Colonel Frank Wolford's First Kentucky troopers were among those moving in for the kill. Deciding that he could not fight his way through Lebanon, Morgan bypassed it on a forced march that started an hour before midnight. While a few companies feinted an attack on the town and burned rail fences to simulate campfires, the main body swung around the town to the Campbellsville road. Men who made that march later described it as their most miserable night of the war. Freezing rain turned to sleet, and coats of ice soon covered men and horses; troopers had to dismount frequently to avoid freezing in the saddle. Men and horses slipped and slid on the treacherous footing through the long night.

But they reached Campbellsville safely and dined there New Year's Eve on captured supplies. Their determined pursuers were still coming on when the Confederate column passed through Columbia on the first day of 1863. During the afternoon they heard the dull rumble of distant artillery fire; although they did not know it then, the sound came from the savage fighting at distant Stone's River, where other Kentuckians played an important role and suffered heavy casualties. Their Union pursuers finally left behind, the Confederates crossed into Tennessee on January 3.

Morgan reported only 2 men killed and 24 wounded. Of the 64 who were missing a number later rejoined the command. He claimed nearly 2,000 Union casualties, including the paroled prisoners, and the destruction of large amounts of military supplies. The impact of the raid on Rosecrans's supply problem was indicated by a telegram from General Horatio G. Wright in Cincinnati to General Boyle in Kentucky: "We must open the railroad soon or Rosecrans will starve." [6]

During the next few months Confederate detachments continued to infiltrate among the Union garrisons trying to protect the state. Colonel Roy S. Clukes's Eighth Kentucky Cavalry crossed the Cumberland on February 18 in bitterly cold weather. For several weeks the 750 Confederates sustained themselves in the Bluegrass although they were under constant threat and frequent attack. General John Pegram, who had been Kirby Smith's chief of staff during the 1862 invasion, led his cavalry brigade into the state and captured Danville on March 24 despite stout resistance from Wolford's command. Pegram withdrew across the Cumberland River after a sharp clash with General Q. A. Gillmore near Somerset on March 30. General Humphrey Marshall drove into eastern Kentucky from his Virginia theater in late March, but Union troops checked him near Louisa. A Confederate raid on Tompkinsville on April 22 resulted in the burning of the courthouse and several other buildings; a week later a Confederate force was driven away from Monticello. On May 11 several hundred soldiers participated in a fight in Wayne County, and on May 13 a skirmish was fought near Woodburn in Warren County.

And the forays continued. Pegram reentered the state and skirmished with Federal troops near Monticello. A small Confederate unit was defeated on Wilson's Creek near Boston on June 13. A raid at Elizabethtown the same day did some damage to L & N rolling stock. Three hundred Confederate cavalry raided Maysville on June 14; Olympia Springs in Bath County was the site of a small action on June 15; a somewhat more extensive engagement was fought near Morehead on June 16. On June 18 Captain Thomas Hines, one of Morgan's advance men, crossed the Ohio River into Indiana with some 65 soldiers. The Union forces could do little but react to the Confederate raids, for the initiative lay with the enemy. It was a period of hard riding and endless frustration for the Union troops, and they may have felt some sense of relief when Morgan raised the level of the raids to a more visible one.

His appetite for fame whetted by the acclaim received for his exploits in Kentucky and Tennessee, Morgan dreamed of still greater glory. Guarding Bragg's right flank during the spring of 1863 was a boring task, the more irksome because under General Wheeler's conservative direction. Morgan must have known that many of his officers and men believed that he had lost much of his dash and verve when he took a bride, and he yearned to refurbish his reputation. Morgan believed in carrying the war to the enemy, and sometime during the late spring he sought Bragg's permission to raid across the Ohio River. Such an excursion, he suggested, would create enough havoc and excitement to tie up thousands of troops that otherwise would go to reinforce Rose-crans. He may also have hoped to make some contact with the underground Copperhead movement in the Old Northwest.

Bragg's army, concentrated around Tullahoma, Tennessee, had been weakened in the effort to save Vicksburg from Grant's relentless advance, and Bragg decided that he must withdraw toward Chattanooga. But a swift move by Rosencrans might catch the Confederates strung out on the march, and thus Bragg was glad to sanction a raid that would divert the Federals' attention elsewhere at the critical moment. Morgan was given permission to lead another raid into Kentucky, but he was ordered not to cross the Ohio River. Morgan had already sent men to scout the fords along the upper Ohio that he might use during their return, and he told Duke that they were going to invade the North regardless of orders. If Lee was still in Pennsylvania, Morgan said, they might even ride to join him instead of returning to Bragg's army. As Duke later wrote, "He did not disguise from himself the great danger he encountered, but was sanguine of success." [7]

In late May, Morgan concentrated his regiments, including the new Fifth Kentucky Cavalry, in the area between Liberty and Alexandria, Tennessee. Remounts were available; supply wagons suddenly appeared; the troops were worked into excellent condition. They were ready to move out by June 11, but a Federal raiding party was reported headed for Knoxville and Morgan was ordered to intercept it. For three miserable weeks the Confederates floundered in mud and rough terrain without ever finding the enemy; when the raid finally started, both men and horses had lost the fine condition Morgan had worked to achieve. But he refused to delay longer, and on July 2, 1863, some 2,460 men crossed the flooded Cumberland River near Burkesville. Boats were scarce, and many of the men stripped off their clothes and swam their mounts across the stream, hanging on to the floating tails. A small group of Union soldiers who chanced to be there were amazed by the sudden attack by naked and half-dressed Confederates.

The Union commanders in Kentucky had been aware of the danger of another sizable Confederate attack. The area along the southern border from the mountains in the east to heavily fortified Bowling Green formed a broad gateway into the state that had already been used many times. Despite his efforts to maintain secrecy, rumors of Morgan's intended raid had seeped into Kentucky. General James M. Shackleford, who had organized the Eighth Kentucky Cavalry in August 1862, had been shifted eastward from Russellville to intercept Morgan if he entered through the southern gateway. General Edward Henry Hobson had predicted Morgan's point of entry almost exactly, but his superior, General Henry M. Judah, had created a gap by ordering Hobson's Second Brigade, Third Division, to move from the vicinity of Columbia to Glasgow.[8]

The Confederates spent the night of July 3 in or near Columbia without encountering serious opposition, but scouts came back to report that the Union garrison at Tebb's Bend on the Green River was alert, well dug in, and prepared to fight. When the Confederates moved up the next day, Morgan made his usual demand for immediate and unconditional surrender. Colonel Orlando Moore had confidence in his Twenty-fifth Michigan Infantry, however; noting that it was Independence Day, he replied cheerfully, "It is a bad day for surrender, and I would rather not." [9] Colonel D. W. Chenault dismounted his men and led the Eleventh Kentucky in a headlong assault that Moore beat off with volleys of rifle fire. Chenault was killed in the futile charge, and when Morgan finally bypassed the position, leaving the defiant Moore in command of the field, the Confederates had suffered seventy-one casualties. It was, perhaps, an omen of the difficulties that lay ahead.

Strong opposition was encountered again the next day

at Lebanon, where Lieutenant Colonel Charles Hanson commanded the Twentieth Kentucky Infantry and detachments from three other Kentucky regiments. Believing that help was on the way, Hanson held out for some time in the brick railroad depot before surrendering. Among the Confederate casualties was Morgan's nineteen-year-old brother, Tom. Since Union troops were reported nearing the town, the Confederates moved out rapidly toward Springfield, their pace impeded by a heavy rainstorm and by the prisoners there had been no time to parole. They splashed on through the wet night and reached Bardstown near daybreak on July 6.

The pursuit was more persistent than Morgan had anticipated. He had often humiliated his opponents, and they were grimly determined that this time the outcome would be different. Fifty-five-year-old Major Starling in Shackleford's command typified the new spirit. At Lebanon on July 6 he penned a hasty note to his daughters: "I am here, we go at once to Bardstown in pursuit of Morgan. Am well, have not pulled off my boots for a week & sleep every night under a tree. Farewell, I know not how this pursuit will end—but I'll be killed or kill some one if we come up with Morgan." When "Lightning" Ellsworth took over the telegraph office at Lebanon Junction, he learned that strong cavalry units were no more than a day behind and that troops were being hastily gathered to protect Louisville from the anticipated attack. Citizens were being enrolled in companies for the defense of the city, and business houses were ordered closed to facilitate the construction of fortifications.[10]

But Morgan had already selected Brandenburg as his crossing point, and he had rushed units on ahead to seize boats there and to make contact with Captain Thomas Hines, the mysterious gentleman who had been scouting possible routes for some weeks and who was reputed to have established contacts with Confederate sympathizers in the Old Northwest. Two companies were sent into the area between Louisville and Frankfort in an effort to convince Union authorities that Morgan was once again moving into the Bluegrass. Such tactics failed to fool the hard-riding pursuers, who maintained their killing pace.

On July 7 the Confederate advance guard captured two river steamers, the *John B. McCombs* and the *Alice Dean,* and embarkation began when the main body arrlved the next morning. A motley crew of local militia and a gallant little gunboat delayed the crossing for an hour, but by midnight all of the Confederates were on the north shore of the Ohio. The advance Union units arrived in Brandenburg just as the crossing was completed.

Intense excitement spread through the Ohio Valley during the next three weeks as the Confederate raiders were chased across southern Indiana and Ohio. Major Starling explained to his daughters why the Union cavalry was not able to close the gap: "We followed him from Burksville steadily, gaining nothing on him, for his scouts took literally every horse within miles of the road, leaving none for us to recruit from, his way was sprinkled with broken down horses left on the road." They would never catch up, Starling complained, "unless some force meets him in front and delays his progress." [11]

By July 19 the flooded fords of the Ohio were guarded by gunboats and troops had been rushed upstream by steamers. The Union cavalry at last caught up, and at Buffington Island, Duke surrendered 700 men after holding out long enough for Morgan and 1,100 others to escape the trap in which they had become ensnarled. More than 300 of the hard-pressed Confederates crossed the deep ford at Belleville, West Virginia, but the others were turned back by the arrival of one of the ubiquitous gunboats. Morgan's command dwindled day by day as exhausted men collapsed, and when he finally surrendered near Lisbon, Ohio, on July 26, 1863, he had only 363 men with him. The long ride was ended, and the Confederates were sent to various prison camps. Wolford and Morgan had served together during the Mexican War, and they shared a deep mutual respect. Wolford conducted Morgan and his officers to Wellsville, where they were to catch a train for Cincinnati. While they waited, he invited them to share a chicken dinner at the hotel and generously extended other hospitality. "Gentlemen, you are my guests," he was reputed to have told the Confederates whom he had chased for several hundred miles. "This hotel together with its bar, cigar stand, and other accessories is at your service and my expense. Do not go off the square in front of the hotel." [12]

Morgan and several of his officers escaped from the Columbus penitentiary in late November, just after the remnants of his command under Adam Johnson had participated in the Confederate defeat at Missionary Ridge. Morgan found Confederate authorities much cooler toward him than they had been in the past, and Bragg threatened to court-martial him for disobeying orders. But because the Confederacy needed leaders desperately, Morgan was restored to command. Although he gradually built up his force, never again did it possess the élan of the outfit that entered Kentucky in July 1863.

During the remainder of 1863 and the early months of 1864 Kentucky was the scene of many small-scale engagements, most of which were officially described as skirmishes. Small Confederate units could slip into the state with little difficulty, and during relatively peaceful interludes Confederate commanders often gave permission for Kentuckians to return to their native state to visit family and friends, to acquire badly needed horses, to harass the Union defenders, and perhaps to gain a few recruits. The harried Union commanders rushed troops hither and yon in vain efforts to rid Kentucky of the Confederate interlopers. As the war lengthened, many of those hunted were guerrillas who had little if any legitimate connection with either army.

During the spring of 1864 the western end of the state was the scene of a more serious raid conducted by Forrest, who had been active in Kentucky during the early days of the war. Commissioned major general in December 1863, Forrest had sought and received an independent command in western Tennessee and northern Mississippi when he found it impossible to serve any longer under Bragg. In the spring of 1864 this legendary warrier decided to raid the western part of Kentucky. One reason for doing so was to secure mounts for some footsore Kentuckians who were tired of marching.

Abraham Buford, an 1841 graduate of West Point, had resigned his commission in 1854 and built a fine stock farm near Versailles. He maintained personal neutrality until 1862, when he accepted a Confederate commission as brigadier general. After serving in the Vicksburg campaign, he was ordered to report to Forrest with the fragments of three Kentucky infantry regiments that had been in Bragg's army. These Kentuckians had requested permission to reorganize as mounted infantry, but the Confederacy could not supply horses for them. Their hope of securing mounts depended upon Forrest's success in his raid.

Forrest started his column on March 15 with nearly 2,800 men, including the Kentucky infantry. Federal General Stephen A. Hurlbut in Memphis exaggerated the size of the Confederate force but was reasonably accurate as to its destination: "It is reported that Forrest, with about seven thousand men, was at Tupelo last night, bound for west Tennessee," he warned; "I think he means Columbus and Paducah." After taking Union City, Tennessee, the Confederates pushed on to Paducah on the Ohio River. Advance units drove the Union troops there aboard gunboats or into the earthwork fort that guarded the western side of the town. Colonel S. G.

Explosion of a gun aboard the *Carondelet* at Fort Donelson, Tennessee, February 1862

Confederate
infantry escaping
from Fort Donelson,
February 1862

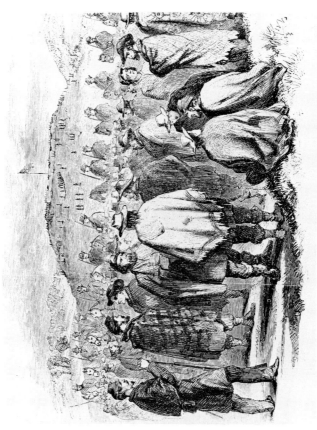

Confederate prisoners
at Fort Donelson,
February 1862

The battle at Green River, September 1862

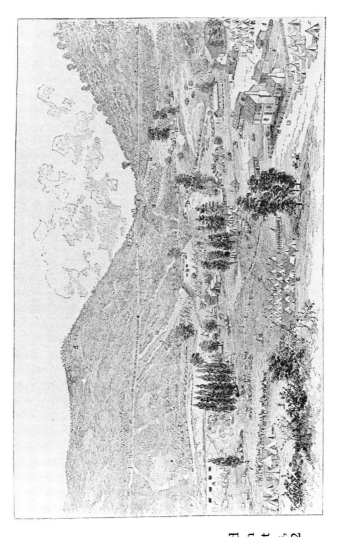

View of Cumberland
Gap from the south
showing encampment
of Union troops,
September 1862

Buell's troops entering Louisville, September 1862

...mmand to some 2,700 men, about one-third of them ...mounted. Although his command area was south-...estern Virginia, Morgan's heart was in the Bluegrass; ...d during the spring some of his scouts drifted into the ...te to ascertain the enemy's strength and dispositions. ...May 31 he informed the War Department that he ...s leaving Wytheville to raid in Kentucky; he was out ...touch with Richmond before he could be ordered to ...turn.

The horseless soldiers delayed the others despite ...ubling up. For a week the column stumbled through ...fficult terrain that one officer maintained had "little ...r man to eat and nothing for horse."[14] The weary sur-...vors reached Mount Sterling in early morning on ...ne 8, and 300 surprised Union soldiers surrendered ...most immediately. Then came the main blemish on ...organ's record. Some of his men and officers got out of ...ntrol, looting the town thoroughly and taking more ...an $70,000 from the bank. Morgan did not order a full ...vestigation when the outrages were called to his at-...ntion, and his reputation was tarnished by rumors that ...had shared in the loot. At the least, he was inexcus-...ly negligent in failing to take prompt, decisive action ...ainst the offenders. Grenfell was gone and Duke was ...ll in a Union prison; they had provided much of the ...scipline in earlier years.

When Morgan moved out toward Lexington, he left ...olonel Henry Giltner's troopers and Lieutenant Colo-...l Robert M. Martin's reluctant infantry behind to de-...roy supplies and search for horses. But General Ste-...en G. Burbridge had learned of the Confederates' ...cation, and their camp was suddenly overrun by ...nion troopers and the Forty-fifth Kentucky Infantry. ...wo hundred fifty Confederates were captured; the rest ...caped because the Federal troops were too exhausted ...y their forced march to take up the pursuit at once. ...organ considered turning back to deal with the threat ...osing in behind him, but he ultimately decided to

72

Reception of Ninth Indiana
Volunteers at Danville,
October 1862

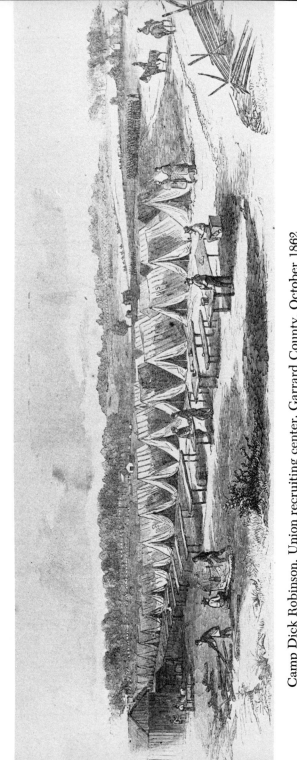

Camp Dick Robinson, Union recruiting center, Garrard County, October 1862

Hicks, commander of the Fortieth Illin[ois?]
665 men and considerable courage; whe[n]
ates demanded unconditional surrende[r]
Forrest's main objectives were horses a[nd]
had no intention of wasting lives by as[sault]
But one of his brigade commanders,
Thompson, a resident of that area, laun[ched]
and futile attack in which he and two d[ozen?]
tuckians were killed or wounded. In h[is]
General Forrest declared: "I . . . drov[e]
their gunboats and fort, and held the tow[n]
. . . Captured many stores and horses;
bales of cotton, one steamer, and the dr[y]
out 50 prisoners." [13]

Most of Forrest's men returned to Te[nnessee]
portion of General Buford's command
disbanded at Mayfield so that the men
homes and secure better clothing and
promised to report to Trenton, Tenness[ee]
and members of the outfit later claimed
returned as promised to his unit. Some
papers carried gleeful stories that the
horses and mules in Paducah had been
that Forrest had obtained only the anim[als]
private citizens. Incensed by this repor[t]
back into Kentucky to get the animals the[y]
to have missed. A small force demonstra[ted]
lumbus to draw Union attention there
main unit arrived at Paducah on April
drove Hicks into the safety of his fort. Th[ey]
found 140 good horses in a foundry, just
pers had reported, and Buford took them
rode southward to rejoin Forrest. In th[ese]
these raids, there was a considerable sha[re]
commanders in western Tennessee and K[entucky]

Soon after Forrest left Kentucky, Morg[an]
in. Despite strong reservations among top
his reliability, Morgan had succeeded in

push on to Lexington, where 5,000 mounts were reported gathered.

Lexington was so poorly guarded that John Castleman, who rode in during the early morning hours, had some difficulty in finding anyone to hear his demand for surrender. After the railroad depot and some military storehouses were burned, the battery guarding the town surrendered. Here also a considerable amount of looting occurred. The Lexington *Observer & Reporter* remarked wryly that although Morgan was there only a few hours, "he made good use of his time, as many empty store shelves and pockets will attest." [15] Morgan took the opportunity for a brief visit to his home; it was the last time that he would ever see it.

The pursuers were closing in, and by midafternoon the Confederates, all of them now mounted, were riding for Georgetown with a herd of extra horses trailing the column. There was more looting in Georgetown. Morgan had lost control over his men, and he was fast losing the confidence of some officers who could not understand or accept his unwillingness to deal with the breakdown in discipline. From Georgetown the Confederates rode through a long night for Cynthiana, which they captured early in the morning of June 11. Much of the town burned during the battle that resulted in 500 prisoners. Morgan wrote Richmond, "The enemy took shelter in the houses, and I was forced to burn a large portion of the town"; [16] but some of his own followers doubted that the fires had been necessary.

Even as the garrison surrendered, word came that General Hobson, who had helped capture Morgan in 1863, was approaching with a large detachment. Somehow the Confederates shook off their fatigue and proved that they were still capable of conducting an operation as they had done so often in earlier years. Giltner engaged the enemy, while Morgan and Colonel D. Howard Smith circled Hobson's flank and charged into his rear. White flags went up almost at once, and the amazed Confederates found themselves with 1,300 prisoners. They posed a new problem, for Union soldiers were now forbidden, under threat of court-martial, to give their paroles. If they were turned loose they would soon rejoin the pursuit, but could they possibly be carried into Confederate lines? Morgan and his officers argued over what should be done. Convinced that other Union troops must be near, Giltner urged immediate departure, even if the prisoners had to be abandoned.

But Morgan insisted that there was no danger, that they would whip Burbridge when he came up, that everyone needed rest, that perhaps some arrangement could be made with the prisoners. His will prevailed, and the troops bedded down for the night. As Giltner made the round of his guardposts, he told an aide that he feared disaster was confronting them. "General Morgan is a very likeable man, and a genius in raiding; but he is such an optimist. I have advised him to leave at once but he persists in remaining and fighting Burbridge's command with near-empty guns. In all probability he will attack us at daybreak tomorrow." [17]

Giltner was right. Burbridge stormed the Confederate camp at dawn on Sunday morning, June 12. The Federals outnumbered the Confederates at least two to one, and some of Morgan's units soon exhausted their ammunition. In the panic that developed, the bridge over the Licking River was jammed with terrified horses and riders. About 250 Confederates were killed or captured, and the rest were so badly scattered that weeks passed before many of them straggled back into Virginia. Morgan reached Abingdon on June 20 with the largest group that escaped, but it was a pitiful remnant of the command with which he had left only three weeks earlier.

Bragg and other Richmond authorities received reports from Kentucky assailing Morgan's actions there, and several of his senior officers asked the War Department to investigate the charges when Morgan stubbornly refused to do so. On August 30 the general was suspended from command and a court of inquiry was ordered for September 10. But when a Union force was reported moving toward Bull's Gap, Morgan ignored his suspension and moved to intercept it; he established his headquarters in Greeneville, Tennessee, on September 3. The Union commanders may have been told by a local Unionist sympathizer that Morgan was spending the night in the town. Early Sunday morning General Alvin C. Gillem's men swarmed into the town, and John Hunt Morgan was killed as he tried to reach his troops. Among those who attended his funeral in Abingdon were the members of the court of inquiry who had convened there to consider his guilt.

Small-scale fighting continued in Kentucky until the end of the war, for there was no way to prevent raiders from slipping into the state. But there was no invasion of real consequence after the spring of 1864, and guerrilla activities that bore little relationship to military operations accounted for much of the continued bloodshed. Although many of the guerrillas claimed some military association, they were an embarrassment to their putative commanders, and their actions were repudiated by the governments they pretended to serve. Champ Clark did not exaggerate when he recalled, "The land swarmed with cutthroats, robbers, thieves, firebugs, and malefactors of every degree and kind, who preyed upon the old, the infirm, the helpless, and committed thousands of brutal and heinous crimes—in the name of the Union or the Southern Confederacy." Citizens were killed, property was stolen or destroyed, and courthouses were burned; no Kentucky county escaped such outrages. W. F. Wickersham expressed the opinion of many Kentuckians toward bushwhackers when he told members of his family, ". . . if you catch one of them I want you to kill the infernal scamps of the earth, they are not fit for no place but hell. . . ." [18]

The most notorious Kentucky guerrilla was probably

"Sue Mundy," who as Captain Jerome Clarke had served in Morgan's command. He returned to Kentucky after his leader's death and began his nefarious career in October 1864. The confusion concerning his identity and the uncertainty over his sex intrigued the public, and Clarke was blamed for depredations he could not have committed. He and two companions, one critically wounded, were captured in a tobacco barn near Brandenburg on March 12, 1865, after an informer told Union authorities of their hideout. Clarke, "alias Sue Mundy," was tried in Louisville by a hastily convened military commission, found guilty, and hanged on the afternoon of March 15 before a crowd estimated at several thousand persons.[19]

William Clarke Quantrill, who had become notorious for his activities in Kansas before and during the war, transferred his attentions to Kentucky in January 1865. He and several dozen heavily armed desperadoes entered the state near Canton and then moved eastward, committing crimes in such communities as Hartford, Hustonville, and Danville. Quantrill may even have joined Sue Mundy for raids on Midway and New Market. A militia company under the determined leadership of Captain J. H. Bridgewater inflicted serious losses on Quantrill's band but failed to destroy it. Then Major General John M. Palmer employed Edwin Terrill, the leader of some Unionist guerrillas in Spencer County, to complete the job. Terrill caught Quantrill at a hideout near Bloomfield on May 10. Severely wounded during his attempted escape, Quantrill died in the Louisville military prison hospital on June 6. His men who had escaped Terrill finally surrendered to an army officer at Wakefield on July 26.[20]

In their efforts to suppress guerrilla activities the Union authorities embarked upon a repressive and at least partially unconstitutional program that aroused a great deal of civilian resentment. In the summer of 1862 General Boyle ordered penalties for anyone who aided the marauders and announced that military commissions would supervise the payment by disloyal persons for damages done to loyal citizens. When some Union men in the Caneyville area were robbed, Confederate sympathizers were assessed $35,000. In 1864 the legislature established fines up to $5,000 and imprisonment up to one year for "disloyal and treasonable practices" and provided "a civil remedy for injuries done by *disloyal* persons." An act of February 22, 1864, allowed double indemnity through civil action for depredation losses. Governor Thomas E. Bramlette promised that the guerrillas would be stopped "even though every arm be required to aid in their destruction," and in January 1864 he ordered five rebel sympathizers arrested and held as hostages for the safe return of any loyal person who might be carried off. A Frankfort editor commented, "We have but one amendment to make to the proclamation, and that is, every guerrilla and marauder who is caught, ought to be hung upon the first tree." [21]

Much of the odium for enforcing the antiguerrilla provisions fell upon General Burbridge, who became commander of the military district of Kentucky on February 5, 1864. It would have been a trying position for anyone, but the thirty-two-year-old farmer from Logan County lacked the experience and tact needed for the job. In his zeal to enforce the laws he antagonized much of the state, including many staunch Unionists. As the officer in charge, he was blamed for the congressional act of July 2, 1864, that gave military courts jurisdiction over the "guerrilla-marauders" and for President Lincoln's suspension of the writ of habeas corpus and invocation of martial law on July 5. Burbridge himself was responsible for instituting an infamous retaliation policy. Four guerrilla prisoners were to be shot for each Union man killed. Some of those executed were apparently legitimate Confederate prisoners of war, and a storm of protest swept the state. After July 16 any Confederate sympathizer within five miles of a guerrilla raid was subject

77

to arrest and banishment from the country. An order of October 26, 1864, to take no more guerrilla prisoners stirred up even more opposition. Men who were believed to have influence with the Union authorities received many pitiful pleas for help. They received scant encouragement from Robert J. Breckinridge, whose own family had divided over the issue of the war. His ministerial studies had evidently been concentrated on the Old Testament, for his stern admonition contained little mercy: "Treat them all alike, and if there are any among them who are not rebels at heart, God will take care of them and save them at least." [22]

Enraged and frustrated by the assistance rendered Confederates who slipped into the state, some Union authorities made little effort to distinguish between loyal and disloyal citizens. A War Department agent, speaking for many military officials in the state, wrote Secretary Edwin M. Stanton in late 1864, "A large majority of Kentuckians are today undoubtedly disloyal." [23] Governor Bramlette frequently protested odious policies and their insensitive enforcement, and he was joined by a wide spectrum of the state's press and public figures. Prolonged efforts by the governor and legislature to secure the removal of General Burbridge finally succeeded in February 1865. The Louisville *Journal* of February 10 carried a brief announcement: "Maj. Gen. John M. Palmer of Illinois had been appointed to command in Kentucky. Thank God and President Lincoln."

Palmer was a more tactful administrator than his predecessor; but since the policies he enforced remained essentially the same, he soon became unpopular in his own right. The end of the war eliminated the most obvious possibilities for discontent, although Kentucky was treated much like a conquered province during the Reconstruction era. Much of Kentucky's postwar bitterness toward the federal government stemmed from the problems that developed during the last two years of the war. Kentucky's resentment of the repressive program and her anger over the freeing of the slaves did much to shape her postwar political stance.

As the long conflict drew to a close, Kentuckians continued to fight on battlefields far distant from the green hills of home. General Duke had some 600 men in his brigade in western Virginia when Lee surrendered at Appomattox. Their horses were not up from winter grazing, and so Duke mounted his men on mules taken from a supply train and headed south to join Joe Johnston's army in North Carolina. Only 10 of his men decided to stay behind, and Duke wrote of his followers, "Braver in the hour of despair than ever before, they never faltered or murmured." After Johnston surrendered, the Kentuckians formed a large part of the escort for President Davis and the remnants of the Confederate government in their flight. A South Carolina lady denounced the "thieving, rascally Kentuckians" who had taken forage from her barn. They were "afraid to go home," she declared, "while our boys are surrendering decently." One of the Kentuckians replied: "Madam, you are speaking out of your turn; South Carolina had a good deal to say in getting up this war, but we Kentuckians have contracted to close it out." [24]

They were true to their contract, remaining with Davis until he decided to attempt escape with a smaller group. Some of the other units then surrendered, but Duke had not received any order to do so. Almost surrounded by much larger Union forces, he waited until Major General John C. Breckinridge, then Confederate secretary of war, sent word for them to yield. Further resistance would be foolish, Breckinridge said. They should return home and take up civilian lives as soon as possible. They were not to make any effort to help him escape: "I will not have one of these young men encounter one hazard more for my sake."

"We communicated his message to our comrades," Duke wrote, "and for us the long agony was over." [25]

5

THE IMPACT
OF THE WAR

Kentucky did not experience as much physical damage as some of the other states in which the war was fought, but there were few citizens of the commonwealth whose lives were not affected in some way by the demands of the great conflict. Kentuckians have long been noted for their unusual political behavior, and the waging of war intensified the political battles at home.

The Unionist legislature elected in 1861 passed a series of measures in late 1861 and early 1862 designed to curb Confederate support and to lend assistance to the Union. Loyalty oaths were required of teachers, ministers, and jurors, in addition to public officials; and severe penalties were provided for any Kentuckian who invaded the state, enlisted in the Confederate army, or enticed anyone else to enlist. A fine of $50 to $100 was levied against anyone who displayed a Confederate flag, and the legislators formally expelled several members who had joined the Confederacy. After the state's neutrality ended, the legislature declared that United States Senators John C. Breckinridge and Lazarus W. Powell "do not represent the will of the people of Kentucky." Breckrinridge resolved the charge by joining the Confederate army; he would be the only Confederate to hold both a cabinet post and a military rank as high as major general. Powell, however, defended himself ably against charges of disloyalty and finally won a 28–11 vote of confidence from his colleagues in Washington.[1]

A particular problem for Kentucky Unionists, as already noted, was the presence of Governor Magoffin, who had been elected in 1859 on the Democratic ticket. Confronted by hostile legislative majorities after the 1861 election, Magoffin could do little more than delay the actions of his Unionist opponents, who overrrode his vetoes with little effort. Well aware of his precarious position, the governor was careful to execute the measures enacted over his objections. In a September message to the legislature he acknowledged his belief in states' rights, but asserted, "My functions are purely executive, and I am bound by my oath of office to carry out the lawful will of the people, whether the policy they prefer accords with my own views or not." [2] As early as September 30 a resolution calling for his resignation was introduced in the Senate. While the resolution died in committee, criticism did not cease.

The legislature stripped the governor of many of his constitutional powers, such as control over the state's military forces; yet he was blamed for the Confederate invasions of the state and for the excesses of General Boyle in enforcing laws that the governor had opposed. His tone was almost plaintive when he asserted, "I have been more untiring in my honest efforts, to preserve, and have made more propositions to prevent, a dissolution of the Union . . . than all of my busy, brawling calumniators, who had their vile purposes to serve." [3] His position became increasingly untenable, and in mid-August 1862 he participated in one of the most unusual political maneuvers in the commonwealth's history.

On August 16 Magoffin informed the legislature that W. A. Dudley, state quartermaster general, had recently inquired if there was any truth to the rumors of his resignation. Dudley urged him to resign, both for his own sake and for the welfare of the state. In his reply, Magoffin told Dudley that certain conditions would have to be met before he could consider such action. "Could I be assured, that my successor would be a conservative, just man, of high position and character, and that his policy would be conciliatory and impartial toward all law-abiding citizens, however much they may differ in opinion; and that the constitutional rights of our people would be regarded, and the subordination of the military to the civil power be insisted on and maintained to the utmost extent our disturbed condition will admit, I would not hesitate an instant in putting off the cares of office, and in tendering him my best wishes for the success of his administration." [4] The snag was that Lieutenant Governor Linn Boyd had died in office, and Speaker of the Senate John F. Fisk, next in line of succession, did not meet Magoffin's requirements. But on August 16 in a bewildering series of moves Fisk resigned as speaker, Senator James F. Robinson was elected unanimously to replace him, and the governor announced his resignation, to be effective at ten o'clock on Monday morning, August 18. In a gesture of cordiality lacking for some time, the legislature invited Magoffin to attend Robinson's inauguration in the house chamber. With the change safely made, Fisk was then reelected to the speakership from which he had so recently resigned.

Another embarrassment for the Unionists was General Boyle, whose zeal often antagonized even members of his own party. Boyle interfered in the 1862 local elections by publishing an order on July 21 that threatened arrest on the charge of treason for any candidate whose opinions were hostile to the national government. The Unionists would have won most of the elections anyway, and the main effect of this blatant interference with the political process was to drive citizens into opposition. The Southern Rights party called for a convention to meet on February 18, 1863, to nominate candidates for state offices; many Unionists were convinced that the real purpose was to promote secession. The House of Representatives refused to allow its premises to be used for the convention, and when the delegates met in Frankfort's Metropolitan Hall, Colonel E. A. Gilbert moved infantrymen to the site. He would not allow disloyal sentiments to be uttered, the colonel declared; nominees would not be permitted to run and, if somehow elected, would be prevented from serving. "Such meetings as this you shall not hold within the limits of my command; . . . you will disperse to your homes, and in future desist from all such efforts to precipitate civil war upon your State." [5] Even the Unionist Senate protested Gilbert's novel approach to the elective process.

The Union Democracy, as its adherents called themselves, held its state convention in Louisville on March 18–19, 1863, with a distinctly military flavor. General Boyle was an active candidate for the nomination for governor, but he had antagonized too many people, and Joshua F. Bell was selected. A month later Bell declined the honor, partly because of poor health, partly because of the dominance of the military in the state. On May 2 the party's central committee replaced him with Thomas E. Bramlette, who had recently resigned from the army because of a dispute over his command. The Union Democrats and their candidate would try to dissociate themselves from the Lincoln administration, but they were inevitably tied to it in the view of many disenchanted Kentuckians.

The result was the formation of another party called the Peace Democrats. In June 1863 several leading politicians, including W. F. Bullock, L. S. Trimble, Joshua F. Bullitt, and W. A. Dudley, asked Charles A. Wickliffe to make the race for governor. They were careful to denounce secession in order to avoid being associated with it: "We hold this rebellion utterly unjustifiable in its inception, and the dissolution of the Union the greatest of calamities. We would see all just and constitutional means adopted to the suppression of the one and restoration of the other." [6] But they attacked the military excesses in the state, and they condemned such measures of the federal government as the Emancipation Proclamation, which had offended many white Kentuckians although it did not apply to the state.

The campaign was bitterly fought, with the Peace Democrats being accused of favoring secession and protecting traitors and the Union Democrats being blamed for the actions of the Lincoln administration and the commonwealth's military authorities. It was a measure of Lincoln's popularity in his native state that both parties sought to dissociate themselves from him and his administration. The *Tri-Weekly Commonwealth* of April 1, 1863, asserted flatly, "No administration man can be elected in Kentucky," and most of the candidates appeared to agree. [7] Bramlette advocated support of the president, but his reasoning was that the sooner the war ended, the sooner the state could get rid of Lincoln's obnoxious policies and measures.

In a proclamation dated July 10 Governor Robinson pointed out that many citizens had been disenfranchised by various war measures and thus should not be allowed to vote. The army intervened actively to prevent the election of Wickliffe and others of his party. Five days before the election General Boyle announced his candidacy for the congressional seat left vacant by the death of John J. Crittenden. In an order dated July 25 the general declared that voting for Wickliffe would constitute sufficient proof of Confederate sympathies to permit the seizure of rebel property. Six days later, General Ambrose E. Burnside, commander of the Department of the Ohio, declared martial law in the state. He did so, he explained, to keep disloyal persons from voting and to make possible a free election. Anyone who attempted to vote without being able to establish his right to do so was to be arrested as a rebel. A formidable barrier was the test oath that was required: "I do solemnly swear that I have never entered the service of the so-called Confederate States; that I have never been engaged in the service of the so-called 'provisional government of Kentucky,' either in a civil or military capacity; that I have never, either directly or indirectly, aided the rebellion against the United States or the State of Kentucky; that I am unconditionally for the Union and the suppression of the rebellion, and am willing to furnish men and money for the vigorous prosecution of the war against the rebellious league known as the 'Confederate States'; so help me God." [8]

The Peace Democracy candidates were kept off the ballot in a number of counties, and in the First District, Judge Trimble, a well-known leader of the party, was held in prison until after the election. Suspected citizens were harassed and often prevented from voting. "Well the election is over, if election it could be called," Maria Knott wrote a few days later. "People had to vote just as the military saw fit or not at all, consequently a small vote was polled. . . . *Not much credit for Ky. remaining union when she cant help herself.*" [9] Bramlette defeated Wickliffe by approximately 68,000 votes to 18,000, and the Union Democrats strengthened their hold on the legislature. Governor Bramlette started his term by voicing strong support for the policies of the federal government, but as he had to cope with the implementation of such policies within the state, his views changed, and he became increasingly opposed to the Lincoln administration.

The presidential election of 1864 also revealed Kentucky's discontent with President Lincoln and his party. The central committee of the Union Democracy decided to send delegates to the national Democratic convention in Chicago instead of the Republican (or Union Party) convention in Baltimore. Robert J. Breckinridge then led a movement to build a party of "true Union men" to counter the claims of the Union Democrats.

The two groups were unable to reconcile their differences, and Breckinridge led his delegation to Baltimore, where he was honored by being elected temporary chairman of the Republican convention. Lincoln was renominated and, in a fateful move to demonstrate national strength, Unionist Andrew Johnson of Tennessee was selected for the vice presidency.

The Union Democratic delegates to the Chicago convention were instructed to support General McClellan for president and Governor Bramlette for his running-mate. The convention condemned the proposed congressional plan of reconstruction, the use of blacks as soldiers, and various alleged usurpations of power by the federal government. The old Southern Rights party of 1860, joined now by the Wickliffe followers, also sent delegates to Chicago under the banner of Peace Democracy. This group favored a great national convention that would attempt to find ways to end the war and reunite the country. The Chicago convention seated both groups and gave each delegate half a vote.

The August 1 state election for minor county officers and the Second District member of the Court of Appeals saw considerable interference by military authorities. Three days before the election General Burbridge ordered Judge Alvin Duvall's name kept off the poll-books; the judge, who had served on the court since 1856, fled the state to avoid probable arrest. Despite the scant time remaining, the Democrats nominated the highly respected George Robertson. At the last moment, too late for Burbridge to prevent his election, they telegraphed his name to the polling places. Although Robertson won, the voter turnout was only about a quarter of those eligible; many voters had apparently been intimidated into forgoing their right of suffrage.

Governor Bramlette led the state's opposition to the highhanded methods employed by General Burbridge and other military leaders to secure Lincoln's election. "I am opposed to your election, and regard a change of policy as essential to the salvation of our country," he informed the president, and protested, "We are dealt with as though Kentucky was a rebellious and conquered province, instead of being as they [*sic*] are, a brave and loyal people." There was little doubt about how Kentucky would vote, despite the efforts of the military. McClellan lost nationally, but he carried the civilian vote of the commonwealth over Lincoln, 61,478 to 26,592, and he also won the separate soldiers' vote, 3,068 to 1,205. Kentucky gave Lincoln his lowest vote (30.2 percent) among the twenty-five states participating in the election. Many Kentuckians obviously felt that Lincoln had abandoned the policy on which the war was being fought; as one newspaper put it, "He has fearfully imperiled the Union cause by his illegal abolition proclamations. . . ." [10]

No other general election was held in Kentucky before the end of the war, but in January 1865 the legislature elected a United States senator. The Radicals, as the Lincoln supporters were beginning to be called, nominated General Lovell H. Rousseau of Louisville, who had taken a strong stand against slavery. James Guthrie, his elderly conservative opponent, won by a surprisingly close vote of 65-56 that may have reflected both concern about Guthrie's age and the good reputation Rousseau enjoyed. The vote was certainly closer than the overall strength of the two state parties at that time. As Kentucky entered the postwar era, the conservative Democrats were the dominant party; the return of Kentuckians who had been fighting in the Confederate armies would add to their strength.

As a member of the Union, Kentucky was expected to supply men for the nation's army. During the early stages of the war, volunteers made up the state's quota of calls issued by the federal government. Minor criminals were allowed to enlist to escape punishment, and women of Unionist sympathies taunted men of military age who stayed at home. But after the bloody campaigns of 1862 the number of volunteers failed to meet the insatiable demand of the army for more bodies. State bounties were not paid in Kentucky as they were in a number of other states, and Frankfort officials had increased difficulty in supplying the numbers requested. The problem was, of course, shared by other states, and on March 3, 1863, Congress passed the first conscription act in the nation's history.

There were cries of outrage in the state against the operation of the act; many of the protests came from those who were subject to the law. But the draft was also attacked as being un-American, degrading to American citizens, and an affront to their patriotism; some critics maintained that it was unconstitutional. Provisions that allowed exemptions for supplying a substitute or paying a $300 commutation fee led to vehement protests that it was "a rich man's war and a poor man's fight." State authorities contended that Kentucky's quota was set too high, since it did not allow for the thousands of men who were in Confederate service, and they charged that the state had not been credited with all of its volunteers. Repeated efforts were made to secure suspension of the act, but the federal government could not afford to give the state such a dispensation.

In fact, relatively few Kentuckians were drafted, although the act was an effective spur to "voluntary" enlistments. The draft of March 1864 was fairly typical. Kentucky was asked to supply 9,186 men. Of that number, only 421 actually rendered personal service; 531 others furnished substitutes; 3,241 paid the $300 commutation charge; and 4,993 dodged the draft. The percentage of draftdodgers became even larger on later calls. Some men hid out in their own neighborhoods; others moved to states where they were not known, and a number fled to Canada or to Europe. Some joined guerrilla bands, and a considerable number decided that if they had to fight, they would prefer to be on the

Confederate side. In February 1865 a Union League of America official wrote that "every draft in Kentucky puts more men in the rebel than in the Union Army." [11]

But the need for troops continued, and the United States gradually turned to an untapped source of manpower—the nation's blacks. Their use created intense excitement in Kentucky. Many Kentucky Unionists were slaveholders, and many more were convinced that the federal government had no right to interfere with slavery within a state. Early suggestions by such public figures as General Frémont and Secretary of War Cameron that slaves should be freed and placed in military service elicited anger and dismay within the state. The legislature demanded the dismissal of Cameron from the cabinet, and General Anderson warned Lincoln that Frémont's proclamations were "producing most disasterous results in this State, and that it is the opinion of many of our wisest and soundest men that, if not immediately disavowed and annulled Ky. will be lost to the Union." [12] Protests were redoubled when similar proposals were advanced in the spring of 1863. No public official in Kentucky endorsed the idea, and most private citizens were bitter in their denunciation of the proposal. Free Negroes were not citizens and they could not be used as soldiers, the editor of the Louisville *Daily Courier* declared on July 14, 1863. The order was simply illegal and would have to be withdrawn.

As a first step that Kentuckians might accept, Lincoln suggested the enrollment of free Negroes, preliminary to their possible future enlistment. This proposal encountered violent opposition, although the number finally available for military service would probably have been well under 1,000. Even General Boyle, who had frequently been at odds with his fellow citizens, objected to the proposal. "You will revolutionize the State," he warned, "and do infinite and inconceivable harm . . . , and it will meet with decided opposition." [13] The opposition was indeed so great that action was postponed until February 1864, when Provost Marshall James B. Fry ordered the enrollment of all blacks of military age, including slaves. A hero of the Union campaigns in Kentucky then brought matters to a head.

Colonel Wolford and his "wild riders" had carved an enviable record in clashes with Morgan and other Confederate raiders; it is doubtful if any other Federal regiment in the state had participated in as many engagements as the First Kentucky Cavalry. Wolford's loyalty and devotion had been unquestioned, but he could not accept the use of black soldiers. In public speeches in Lexington and Danville on March 10 he called for the use of force to prevent their enrollment. He advocated that enrolling officers should be tossed into the penitentiary, and he pledged the support of his troops to block the policy of the federal government. Wolford was arrested and sent to Tennessee for a trial, but his case was finally handled by a dishonorable dismissal from the army he had served so well. Governor Bramlette was as adamant as the colonel. On March 12 he informed the provost marshal in Boyle County, "if the president does not, upon my demand, stop the negro enrollment, I will. I am awaiting his answer." Kentucky faced the most serious internal crisis since the struggle over secession in 1861.

But on March 15, after a series of mysterious conferences involving such Unionists as Robert J. Breckinridge and General Burbridge, the governor issued a conciliatory proclamation calling upon the citizens to avoid "acts of violence" and "unlawful resistance." What had been called for was enrollment of the blacks, not actual enlistment, the governor explained, and protests should be made in a lawful manner. Breckinridge later said that Bramlette had prepared an earlier proclamation that called for armed resistance with Confederate aid; the governor denied that any such statement had ever been drafted.[14] Prentice's *Journal* charged in the March 22 issue that the radicals wanted a confrontation between the state and the federal government so that Kentucky could be "declared in insurrection, her chosen authorities set aside as disloyal, her slaves proclaimed free, her constitution pronounced void, and the revolutionary work of framing a new constitution and of organizing a new government put exclusively in the hands of the radical faction. . . ."

Bramlette led a protest delegation to Washington and extracted Lincoln's promise that blacks would not be enlisted in any county that met its quota through white enlistments. The blacks who were enlisted, the president promised, would be trained out of state. But quotas were not met, and on April 18, 1864, General Burbridge began statewide black enlistments. Loyal slaveholders were to receive up to $300 for each slave lost to the army. Blacks volunteered quickly for a time; when the number dwindled, fugitive slaves were rounded up and pressed into service if their masters approved. Lieutenant Governor R. T. Jacob and ex-Colonel Wolford, now commander of the state troops, led the opposition to the policy. Wolford was arrested in July for disloyalty and attempts to prevent enlistments, but he refused to halt his activities. After the November election both Jacob and Wolford were arrested.

Release them, Bramlette demanded of Lincoln. "For if men of less prudence and patriotism were thus dealt with, having the power they possess, the consequences would be serious indeed. . . . Better send their accusers off; for they will not help us in the day of battle, and Jacob and Wolford will." [15] Lincoln pardoned the two offenders, but Jacob was nearly a month late arriving to preside over the Senate, and the arbitrary arrests further antagonized the public. Negro enlistments continued, however, and by April 1866, when the last of the blacks in the state were demobilized, some 29,000 had been enlisted, nearly 20,000 of them before the end of the war.

The Confederacy had resorted to conscription a year

earlier than the Union, but for obvious reasons the Confederates were not able to set up draft machinery in Kentucky. In its last desperate moments the Confederate government authorized the use of black soldiers, but only a few companies were raised (in Virginia) and none saw active duty.

The future of slavery also aroused intense interest in the state. While the 1860 Republican platform was adamant about preventing the expansion of slavery, it did not call for abolition in states where slavery was legal. Despite his personal opposition to slavery, as the price of union Lincoln was willing to accept an amendment to the Constitution that would protect it in the states that elected to retain it. But as the war continued, Lincoln became convinced that the institution of slavery must be attacked, his justification being that it was an essential war measure.

There had been unrest in Kentucky because certain antislavery army officers were reluctant to return fugitive slaves to their masters. Further, the army's growing demand for slave labor—a demand that soon resembled a draft in many respects—kindled fear in the hearts of many slaveholders. Their concern deepened when President Lincoln suggested that the Border States demonstrate their loyalty by freeing their slaves. On March 6, 1862, he recommended that Congress provide compensation to encourage the states to follow his suggestion. At $400 each, the president wrote the editor of the New York *Times*, the cost of only eighty-seven days of fighting would free all the slaves in Kentucky, Delaware, Maryland, Missouri, and the District of Columbia.[16] Kentucky officials indignantly spurned the proposal, and there is little doubt but that they accurately reflected majority opinion in the commonwealth.

The Confederate retreat from the bloody ground at Antietam permitted Lincoln to issue his preliminary Emancipation Proclamation without its appearing to be a desperate effort to gain additional support in the North and abroad. While the proclamation applied only to those states or areas still in rebellion as of January 1, 1863, Kentuckians were alarmed by the principles upon which it rested, and few citizens of the state endorsed it. W. F. Wickersham, for example, wrote from near Vicksburg, where he was serving in the Union army: "I don't believe that our army will hold together under the circumstances as Mr. Lincoln had made them for our army is not a going to fight to free the Negroes." Others asserted that if the proclamation had been issued a year earlier, Kentucky would have joined the Confederacy. If some slaves could be freed now, the rest could be freed at some future date. Governor Robinson denounced the proclamation in his January 1863 message to the legislature, and the legislators' main problem was to find the wording that would best express their disapproval. There was some wild talk of recalling all Kentuckians who were in the Union army, and a small vocal minority even advocated secession. The situation was so tense that Lincoln hesitated to supply arms for the Home Guard because the reactions of the state's leaders "admonish me to consider whether any additional arms I may send there are not to be turned against the government." [17]

Lincoln was anxious to get emancipation in his native state. If Kentucky would adopt a scheme of compensated emancipation, it would solve the slavery problem in an important state and would encourage emancipation in the other loyal slave states. He urged such a policy upon a group of Kentucky Unionists who visited him in November 1862, and they promised to establish two emancipationist papers to counteract the influence of the Louisville newspapers.[18] But the governor and the legislature scornfully rejected all such proposals. An act of March 2, 1863, forbade any Negro who claimed to have been freed by the Emancipation Proclamation to enter the state; violators were to be seized and treated as runaway slaves. As the war turned against the Confederacy, the end of slavery became inevitable, and the price of slaves in Kentucky declined sharply. On January 31, 1865, Congress completed passage of the proposed Thirteenth Amendment that would end slavery throughout the nation and sent it to the states for ratification. Governor Bramlette recommended ratification, contingent upon Kentucky's receipt of $34,000,000, the assessed value of the state's slaves in 1864. But there was no chance of such conditions being met, and both houses rejected the amendment. When the Thirteenth Amendment became effective in December 1865, Kentucky still clung defiantly to her discredited institution. Her stubbornness had forfeited any opportunity for even partial compensation, and the loss of her slaves was perhaps the state's most serious economic setback of the war years.

When freedom finally came, few of Kentucky's slaves had been prepared for their new status. Years later Will Oats recalled the mingled joy and apprehension with which his people received the news: "They were all very happy, but they were wondering what they were going to do without a home, work, or money." Many of the freedmen continued to work at least temporarily for their former masters. Mrs. Susan Dale Sanders had served in a household near Taylorsville. My mistress "told me I was free after the war was over," Mrs. Sanders said. "I got happy and sung but I didn't know for a long time, what to be free was, as after the war she hired me and I stayed on doin' all the cookin' and washin' and all the work, and I was hired to her for four dollars a month." [19] Their failure to anticipate the end of slavery and to prepare for it caused Kentuckians many problems during the postwar era.

Civil War statistics are notoriously inaccurate, and it is impossible to ascertain with precision Kentucky's manpower contributions to the war. The total enlistment of blacks and whites in Union service probably exceeded 90,000; if the Home Guard is included, the number passed 100,000. Estimates of the number of Kentuckians in Confederate service range from 25,000 to 40,000. With Union and Confederate enlistments combined, Kentucky's proportionate contribution of men was probably as great as that of any state on either side. Perhaps a third of the total died of battle wounds or disease during the war, and many others were crippled for normal civilian life. A state census reported that in October 1864 Kentucky had 21,000 fewer white males over twenty-one years of age than had been in the state in 1861.

Kentucky did not endure the physical destruction inflicted upon several other states, although a number of towns suffered considerable damage. But economic losses were certain when troops passed through a region, and the color of their uniforms made little difference. Fences were burned for firewood, fruit and roasting ears vanished, fodder and grain disappeared, hogs and chickens were never seen again, and horses and mules volunteered for military service. Unionist Joseph Younglove complained to his brother James in April 1862, after the Confederates had evacuated Bowling Green, "We only got our cow about 10 days ago. Some of the Federal soldiers took her out of Tom Calvert's stable and had been milking her until she was found." He had protested the disappearance of fenceposts to the provost marshal: "I told him I thought it hard after the rebels had taken every thing but the posts that friends should take them. . . ." (The posts were returned.) Joseph said that his house and garden had experienced little harm while occupied by Confederate General Buckner, but Union soldiers had broken into his drugstore at least twenty times and done $1,000 worth of damage. Fortunately, Aunt Minerva, a slave, had kept Yankee looters out of his house. Miles Kelly of the Bristow community in Warren County filed claims against the United States government for $17,755.80 for supplies furnished Federal troops. They included 4,648 bushels of corn, 6,070 bushels of oats, 80 tons of hay, and pasture for 550 horses for 70 days.[20]

The state's Shaker communities at Pleasant Hill and South Union were famous for their fine crops and excellent livestock, and they were visited frequently by detachments from both armies. The South Union journal recounted frequent visits such as the one that occurred December 19, 1861. "The Southern Pickets rode up about seven o'clock at night and called for supper to be prepared for four hundred soldiers. We were to have it ready by eight o'clock. . . . After working hard and getting the victuals cooked they did not arrive at the appointed time but came about midnight with five hundred cavalry all expecting supper." [21] South Union never recovered its prewar prosperity.

Of course, payment was sometimes given for the property taken; in that case it was much better to be visited by Union than by Confederate soldiers. Confederate money was difficult to dispose of under the best of circumstances, and its value declined drastically during the war. The demands of the Union army and the Northern civilian population were almost insatiable, and there was a market for almost anything that could be produced or manufactured in the state. Thus the drastic curtailment of the prewar Southern market did not damage the state's economy as it would have under normal conditions. Kentucky was spared most of the desolation that blighted many parts of the Confederacy; she shared in much of the wartime prosperity that pervaded the North after an initial period of depression in 1861. The Northern wholesale farm price index of 100 in 1860 slipped to 97 in 1861, then rose to 112 in 1862, 147 in 1863, 210 in 1864, and fell to 192 in 1865 with the termination of the fighting. The general price index for the same years, starting at 100 in 1860, was 99, 111, 135, 182, and 179.[22]

The demands of the army and a decline in immigration contributed to a shortage of labor that pushed up wages, but at a slower rate than the rise in prices. Thus while nonagricultural wages in the Union rose 43.1 percent between 1860 and 1865, there was a decline in real purchasing power of approximately one-third. As usual in a period of inflation, people living on fixed incomes suffered most severely. Families of Union soldiers were often in dire straits, since privates received only $13 per month during most of the war. The last pay raise of May 1, 1864, brought the amount only to $16, and payments frequently ran as much as six months in arrears. Confederate pay was only $11 per month until June 1864, when it was increased to $18, but inflation had eroded most of its value by then. Kentucky dependents of Confederate soldiers could count on little or no financial assistance. Lieutenant Frank Tryon wrote his wife, Julia, from Murfreesboro about his concern for her economic plight: "I fear that you may be in want and I know of no way to send you money. What we get here would be of no value with you and I can find no way of exchanging it." [23]

During the early months of the war, neutral Kentucky was a major conduit for the transportation of goods southward as the volume of trade suddenly ballooned. The Louisville and Nashville Railroad was the most important single avenue of shipment. While the line had been called completed before hostilities began, the claim was not altogether accurate. Much work, particularly ballasting, remained to be done, and the available equipment was inadequate for the demands suddenly made upon it. When Fort Sumter was fired on, the line had only 30 locomotives, 28 passenger cars, and 297 freight cars to service 269 miles of track. The problem was compounded by the uneven distribution of traffic; the great bulk of goods moved southward with largely empty cars hauled northward. Unionists both within and without the state objected to traffic with the enemy, and Cincinnati officials, always aware of their city's trade rivalry with Louisville, made strenuous efforts to interdict the abnormal flow of traffic to Louisville. Indiana and Illinois authorities also attempted to curtail the consignment of goods through Louisville unless the loyalty of the consignee could be established.

Lincoln was reluctant to cut off the trade for fear hasty action might tip Kentucky's sympathies toward the Confederacy, but such free trade could not be tolerated indefinitely after the war started. Secretary of the Treasury Salmon P. Chase issued an order on May 2, 1861, directing the seizure of "arms, munitions of war, provisions, or other supplies" whose ultimate destination was believed to be "any port or place under insurrectionary control," but the wording was so vague that it had little effect. The Cincinnati *Gazette* of June 15 editorialized bitterly, "The 'neutrality' of Kentucky seems to consist in perfect freedom to furnish our enemies the wherewith to make war upon us, and the Government knowingly permits this nefarious business to go on." [24]

The Union occupation of Cairo, Illinois, cut off a great deal of river traffic and exerted even more pressure on the overburdened L & N. Kentuckians protested loudly as the prohibitions became both more numerous and more effective, and ingenuity was taxed to its limits to discover subterfuges that could circumvent the growing maze of restrictions. After June 24 no shipments could be made from Louisville without a permit from the customs officer, but wagons hauled goods to towns to the south of the city from which they could be loaded without interference. Border towns such as Franklin experienced a sharp increase of imports, with the surplus soon crossing the Tennessee line.

After Kentucky entered the war, the L & N suffered considerable damage and frequent disruption from Confederate raiders, as has been seen in earlier chapters. Strategic bridges and trestles had to be rebuilt time after time, and before the Confederates abandoned Bowling Green, they destroyed the important enginehouse and machine shops as well as the railroad bridge across the Barren River. During the fiscal year ending June 30, 1863, the railroad had its full line in use for only seven months and twelve days. But it was within the Union lines during most of the rest of the war, and the occasional guerrilla raids did comparatively little damage when measured against the organized depredations earlier in the war.[25]

The early stages of the war also witnessed a large increase of river traffic on such streams as the Cumberland, Tennessee, and Green. Goods that reached Columbus could be shipped down the Mississippi to Confederate destinations with little danger of being intercepted. Some of the first effective efforts to halt the movement of goods came from Confederate, not Union, authorities. By acts of May 21 and August 2, the Confederate Congress banned the exportation of cotton, tobacco, sugar, and other products through Kentucky and the other border states. The Union restrictions, while irksome, were not then nearly so stringent. The end of Kentucky's neutrality and the march southward of the Union armies altered the economic situation within the state. Restrictions were enforced more effectively than they had been previously, and some Kentuckians were soon complaining that they were treated as if they were Confederates. Permits were required for most goods and passengers, and such documents could be obtained only by staunch Unionists. Burbridge and other Federal officers later used similar permits to regulate trade within the state to the detriment of anyone suspected of Confederate inclinations.

Among the obnoxious restrictions was one that prohibited merchants in towns under 20,000 population from purchasing more than $3,000 worth of food supplies each month or stocking more than a two-month supply. Governor Bramlette complained to the president that "many *loyal men* are driven out of business . . . for no other reason than their political preferences," and in his January 1865 message to the legislature the governor denounced the permit system as "a most shameful and corrupt system of political partisan corruption and oppression." [26] Kentuckians were especially angered by the refusal of army officers to honor a January 8, 1864, pronouncement of the Treasury Department that all trade restrictions in Kentucky had been rescinded.

While all sections of the state were subject to some economic interference, the western counties that comprised the First Congressional District were hardest hit. Suspected, with considerable justification, of Confederate inclinations and isolated from the central portion of the state, the district's inhabitants were subjected to severe restrictions from the onset of the war. The proscriptions were most severe during the tenure of General E. A. Paine in the summer of 1864. Backed by Paducah's Union League of America, Paine embarked on July 19 on what has been called "a fifty-one days' reign of violence, terror, rapine, extortion, and military murder." [27] He even taxed the United States mail, until the arrival of an investigating committee forced him to flee into Illinois. The army later reprimanded the general for his misconduct, a "punishment" that infuriated his numerous victims.

The "Great Hog Swindle" of 1864 was the major economic scandal of the war in Kentucky. It began in Louisville when Major Henry C. Symonds, depot commissary, declared that he could save money for the government by buying hogs directly from Kentucky farmers and packing the pork for the army without going through the usual contractors. Speculation in pork had driven prices so high that Symonds was given permission to proceed. Convinced that the pork speculators and packers had united against him, the major awarded bids illegally to businessmen who promised to cooperate. To insure an adequate supply of animals, he secured an order from General Burbridge prohibiting any a secessionist, and both of their sons fought for the Confederacy. One can imagine the father's anguish when he announced in the October 2, 1862, issue that his son William had "perished in the cause of the rebellion" from wounds received at Augusta, Kentucky. Prentice never faltered in his opposition to the Confederacy, but he also opposed abolition, and he castigated Lincoln for his Emancipation Proclamation and other acts. Still, he was a solid bedrock of Unionist strength.

Prentice's great rival during the neutrality era was Walter N. Haldeman, whose Louisville *Courier* was an outspoken advocate of the Confederate cause. Excluded from the mails and then suppressed when neutrality ended, the *Courier* was published in Bowling Green until the Confederate evacuation of that town forced it into a sporadic existence inside the Confederacy. It is ironic that in 1868 the *Courier* and the *Journal* combined to form one paper. Less outspoken than Haldeman, John H. Harney, editor of the Louisville *Democrat*, became the voice of the Peace Democrats; he grew increasingly critical of Lincoln and his policies. The Frankfort *Commonwealth* was a consistent supporter of the Unionist cause; the *Kentucky Yeoman*, which had supported secession, modified its views sufficiently that it avoided suppression. A number of small newspapers were victims of wartime shortages and high prices or were suppressed by the army.

The Civil War created an aura of excitement and suspense, and Kentuckians sought relief from the tensions of the war in numerous social activities. Whenever military conditions permitted, the presence of troops led to feverish rounds of dances, parties, band concerts, picnics, flirtations, and, occasionally, weddings. Of course, such activities were usually boycotted by those of opposing political views. Federal troops were taken somewhat for granted, but the entrance of a Confederate detachment into a town with Confederate sympathies

104

shipment of hogs out of state without a permit. A storm of protest greeted the scheme. Symonds and others were accused of "trying to enrich themselves at the expense of helpless Kentucky farmers." Under heavy public pressure, Symonds gradually backed down, Burbridge rescinded his out-of-state order on November 27, and the project was closed before the end of the year. Symonds insisted that he had saved at least $200,000 for the government; Governor Bramlette declared that Kentucky farmers had been robbed of $300,000.[28]

Louisville, which did not incur damage from Confederate raids, after an initial slump prospered more from the war than any other Kentucky city. "Louisville is played out," one overly pessimistic businessman had moaned in the fall of 1861, ". . . all trade is at a standstill. . . . Houses vacated by the dozens, streets looking every day in the week like Sunday, & mens faces like *yardsticks* are few of the troubles, staring every man in the face in this city." [29] His exaggerated description did not remain even partially true for long. With an 1860 population of 69,729, Louisville was by far the commonwealth's largest city and most important trade center. The Louisville and Nashville transportation artery was of great economic value, and the presence of substantial numbers of Union troops both taxed the resources of the community and enhanced its profits. After the Mississippi River was opened by Union armies in 1863, there was a sharp increase in river traffic, although some military restraints continued in effect until the end of the war. A joyous event was the arrival in Louisville on Christmas Eve 1863 of a cargo of molasses and sugar from New Orleans; it was the first such cargo to dock in over two years.

Farmland in the state decreased by 4,000,000 acres during the war, largely because of the scarcity of labor; but higher prices for nearly all produce brought unwonted prosperity to many farmers. By 1864 tobacco was selling for a dollar and a half to two dollars a pound,

101

and cotton grown in the state was bringing up to eighty cents a pound. Land was valued at $225,000,000 in 1861; the total dropped to $174,000,000 the following year, with the probable loss of slaves and the general shortage of labor being at least partly responsible. But by 1865 the figure had climbed to $198,000,000 despite the imminent end of slavery. The decrease in livestock has sometimes been cited as an example of the farmers' economic losses. The 388,000 horses reported in 1861 had dropped to 299,000 by October 1865; the number of mules declined from 95,000 to 58,000 during the same period; the 692,000 head of cattle diminished to 520,000. But it might be more correct to attribute such declines to the unprecedented demand for animals that tempted breeders to sell at abnormally high prices a much larger than usual proportion of their stock.

Few Kentuckians remained unaffected by the war, and the sharp divisions of opinion inevitably "left some permanent cracks in community solidarity that remained a bitter legacy of the Civil War." A Union soldier from Muhlenberg County swore that after the war he could not live with the Confederates near his home: "One or the other of us will have to leave the country forever." A visitor to Albany who watched a Unionist parade there in the summer of 1861 commented, "A Secessionist is not allowed to open his mouth." A Lebanon woman, who did not like Lincoln but could not stand the "traitorous rebels," told a friend that she did not go out much because of the bad feelings between secessionists and Unionists, and Harriet Means of Ashland remarked, "I would not *dare* to give a large party now for fear the ladies would all get into a free fight." In 1862 Georgetown College even refused to graduate a young Mr. Black because he was "a violent secessionist." [30] Some of the state's famous postwar feuds were based at least partly on wartime animosity.

Congregations that had survived the strains and stresses of disagreement over slavery often split apart on the issue of secession. Another religious consequen[ce] the war and the end of slavery was the separati[on] black members from the congregations of which had been a segregated part. Within a few years afte[r] coming of peace, most blacks worshiped in their churches. Concern was sometimes expressed for the verse effect that military service had upon the moral some Kentucky soldiers. "Some that I thought would good boys have gone Astray," one devout soldier c[om]plained, "the Cards is used in place of the testament."

The belated educational progress fostered by Rob[ert] J. Breckinridge during his 1847–1853 tenure as superi[n]tendent of education was a wartime casualty. The co[n]cept of public schools was not firmly established in Ke[n]tucky minds, and little priority was given th[e] educational system during the war. Teachers went int[o] military service or found more profitable undertaking[s] than teaching, and many undernourished school[s] quietly expired. Superintendent of Public Instruction Robert Richardson declared in his 1861 report that the war had "reduced the number of children in attendance on our public schools from 165,000 to about 90,000. An annual school fund, from all sources, of about $340,000 has been reduced by it in a brief period to but little upwards of $200,000." By 1862 the situation was even worse. Some recovery was achieved in 1863, but a year after the war ended the educational statistics were just regaining prewar levels. Colleges were especially hard hit, since many of their students were of military age. Transylvania, only a few decades earlier one of the largest and best colleges in the country, had its buildings converted into a military hospital.

The Civil War inspired little creative activity of note within the state. The most influential writing was found in the state's partisan newspapers that did much to formulate and express public opinion. Prentice, editor of the Louisville *Daily Journal*, was the most important editorial supporter of the Union cause. Yet his wife was

provoked a frenzied celebration before the raiders had to move on. It was a singing war, and soldiers and civilians of all parties wept through lachrymose renditions of "Lorena," "All Quiet Along the Potomac Tonight," "Just Before the Battle, Mother," and "Juanita," while "Dixie" and "The Bonnie Blue Flag" or "John Brown's Body" and "The Battle Hymn of the Republic" betrayed political affiliations. All Kentuckians claimed "My Old Kentucky Home."

If troops remained in an area for an extended period, social activities became better organized and assumed a formal complexion. Bowling Green was the center of Confederate social life during the few months that it was the capital. A local girl was delighted to receive a formal invitation: "The officers of Wirt Adams' Cavalry will be glad to see Miss _____ at a collation at their camp at two o'clock tomorrow afternoon to meet Mrs. Wirt Adams." As a public display of their martial skills, officers often staged dress parades, drills, and sham battles. One sham attack at Bowling Green nearly turned into tragedy when a mistaken order sent 1,200 cavalrymen in a wild charge toward the civilians who were watching the proceedings. Agatha Strange of Bowling Green recalled later: "Our house in those days was visited and made the home of by the intellect and chivalry of the South. . . . These were days of happiness and never can be erased from my memory." [32]

Lieutenant William P. Davis, an engaging young scamp, was one of many soldiers who sampled Kentucky's hospitality during the war. When the Fourteenth Mississippi Infantry entered Hopkinsville on October 1, 1861, Davis capitalized on the warm welcome that greeted the Confederates. "The streets were crowded with ladies, secession flags flying, ladies hunting sick to take care of them," he wrote in his diary. "As I felt very bad and wanted something nice to eat, Charles Williams of Comp K and Segt. Burk and myself concluded we would make a bold start so we asked a negro where

105

some nice young ladies [were] and he carried us to Mr. Dillards where we found three beautiful young ladies. Introducing ourselves as Miss. soldiers, we were invited to take seats and they discoursed some nice music for us and prepared fine supper though I must confess I felt a little bad setting down to a gent's table with ladies for neither of us had changed clothes for 7 days. . . ." A few weeks later Davis and two enlisted friends sought companionship in Bowling Green, where they "found quite a number of ladies at the baptist church preparing to give a tableaux for the benefit of sick soldiers. The ladies asked me to take a part but I excused my self though formed the acquaintance of Miss Dearing, enjoying my self very much and saw Miss Dearing home." Lieutenant Davis at least partly repaid his social obligations to the commonwealth by taking the regimental band into town to give a concert.[33]

Memories of the Civil War have never been erased from the minds of Kentuckians, and for those who lived in that era "the War" was one of the momentous experiences of their lives. They were never quite the same afterwards. Nor was Kentucky ever again quite the same. It is a cliché to say that wars never solve anything; like many clichés, it is not entirely true. Kentuckians who lived into the postwar era discovered that several questions had been settled by that conflict. Limits were set to the doctrine of states' rights; no state has attempted secession since 1861. Slavery was ended in 1865, although a majority of the state's citizens deplored the act. And the heritage of the war and the bitterness engendered during the Reconstruction era led the state into the Southern Democratic ranks for years to come. It has been said with considerable truth that Kentucky joined the Confederacy after the war was over.

Notes

Chapter 1

1. *Eighth Census* (1860): vol. 2, *Agriculture*, 62–63, 184–87; vol. 3, *Manufactures*, 729.

2. Lincoln to Orville H. Browning, Sept. 22, 1861, Roy P. Basler, ed., *The Collected Works of Abraham Lincoln*, 9 vols. (New Brunswick, N.J., 1953–55), 4:532.

3. Jasper B. Shannon and Ruth McQuown, *Presidential Politics in Kentucky, 1824–1948* (Lexington, 1950), 32–35.

4. Sept. 25, Nov. 8, 17, 1860.

5. Wickliffe to Lewis E. Harvie, Nov. 13, 1860, Miscellaneous Papers (The Filson Club, Louisville).

6. *House Journal* (Dec. 1859–Mar. 1860 session), Dec. 6, 1859, 35; Frankfort *Tri-Weekly Yeoman*, Dec. 13, 1860.

7. *House Journal* (called session, Jan.–Apr. 1861), Jan. 17, 1861, 28–32.

8. *House Journal* (called session, Jan.–Apr. 1861), Jan. 17, 1861, 6–11; Frankfort *Tri-Weekly Yeoman*, Dec. 29, 1860, Jan. 18, 1861.

9. Lewis and Richard H. Collins, *History of Kentucky*, 2 vols. (Covington, 1874), 1:87.

10. John J. Crittenden to George B. Crittenden, Apr. 30, 1861, John Jordan Crittenden Letters (The Filson Club). George became a Confederate general; his brother Tom, a Union general.

11. Shackleford to Nelson, May 19, 1861, William Nelson Papers (The Filson Club).

12. A. M. Starling to Mary Starling Payne, May 6, 1861, Lewis-Starling Collection, (Kentucky Library, Western Kentucky University, Bowling Green).

13. Aug. 16, 1861, quoted in E. Merton Coulter, *The Civil War and Readjustment in Kentucky* (Chapel Hill, N.C., 1926),

103; Lincoln to Magoffin, Aug. 24, 1861, Basler, ed., *Works of Lincoln*, 4:497.

14. *House Journal* (Sept.–Oct. 1861 session), Sept. 13, 1861, 101–2; *Senate Journal*, Sept. 13, 1861, 99–100.

Chapter 2

1. Sherman to Lincoln, Oct. 10, 1861, *The War of the Rebellion: A Compilation of the Official Records of the Union and Confederate Armies*, 128 vols. (Washington, D.C., 1880–1901), ser. 1, vol. 4, 300; Thomas to Simon Cameron, Oct. 21, 1861, ibid., 313–14.

2. Oct. 16, 1861, ibid., 308.

3. Quoted in Ezra J. Warner, *Generals in Gray* (Baton Rouge, La., 1959), 160.

4. Martha Lucas Graham to C. Fontaine Alexander, Sept. 15, 1861, Alexander Collection (Kentucky Library); Lowell H. Harrison, "Confederate Kentucky: The State That Almost Was," *Civil War Times Illustrated* 12 (Apr. 1973):16.

5. Lt. Col. George P. Jouett to mother, Feb. 16, 1862, Small Collections, no. 52, (Kentucky Library).

6. Oct. 22, 1861, *Official Records*, ser. 1, vol. 4, 469.

7. Mary _____ to Mary [Hooe Wallace], Oct. 7, 1861, Edmund T. Halsey Collection, folder 30 (The Filson Club).

8. A. C. Quisenbery, "The Alleged Secession of Kentucky in 1861," *Register of the Kentucky State Historical Society* 15 (May 1917):17, 18.

9. Ibid., 18–20.

10. *Official Records*, ser. 1, vol. 7, 857.

11. Report of Thomas, Jan. 31, 1862, ibid., 79.

12. Raymond E. Myers, *The Zollie Tree* (Louisville, 1964), 96; R. M. Kelly, "Holding Kentucky For the Union," Robert Underwood Johnson and Clarence Clough Buel, eds., *Battles and Leaders of the Civil War*, 4 vols. (New York, 1887–88), 1:388–89.

13. Thomas to Buell, Jan. 23, 1862, *Official Records*, ser. 1, vol. 7, 563–64; Johnston to General Samuel Cooper, Jan. 22, 1862, ibid., 844.

14. Quoted in Thomas Lawrence Connelly, *Army of the Heartland* (Baton Rouge, La., 1967), 112.

15. *Official Records*, ser. 1, vol. 7, 161; Arndt M. Stickles,

Simon Bolivar Buckner (Chapel Hill, N.C., 1940), 164–66, 173.

16. Mrs. Albert Covington to Robert William Wells, Mar. 2, 1862, Covington Letter; Alfred Pirtle Journal, Feb. 18, 1862, Alfred Pirtle Papers (The Filson Club).

Chapter 3

1. Collins, *History of Kentucky*, 1:102.

2. Ibid.

3. Quoted in Dee Alexander Brown, *The Bold Cavaliers* (Philadelphia, 1959), 72.

4. July 13, 1862, Basler, ed., *Works of Lincoln*, 5:322; Boyle to Nelson, July 18, 1862; Fennell to Nelson, July 18, 1862, Nelson Papers.

5. Quoted in Brown, *Bold Cavaliers*, 85–86.

6. Report of George A. Ellsworth, July 30, 1862, *Official Records*, ser. 1, vol. 16, pt. 1, 780.

7. Stephen Z. Starr, *Colonel Grenfell's Wars* (Baton Rouge, La., 1971), 54.

8. *Official Records*, ser. 1, vol. 16, pt. 2, 995.

9. Nelson to editors of Cincinnati *Gazette*, Sept. 1, 1862, Nelson Papers.

10. Samuel M. Starling to daughters, Sept. 5, 12, 1862, Lewis-Starling Collection.

11. Shelby Foote, *The Civil War: Fort Sumter to Perryville* (New York, 1958), 657.

12. Report of Col. John T. Wilder, Sept. 18, 1862, *Official Records*, ser. 1, vol. 16, pt. 1, 960.

13. Marmaduke B. Morton, "Last Surviving Lieutenant General: Visit to the Home of Gen. S. B. Buckner," *The Confederate Veteran* 17 (Feb. 1909):95.

14. Samuel C. Williams, *General John T. Wilder* (Bloomington, Ind., 1936), 62; *Official Records*, ser. 1, vol. 16, pt. 1, 962.

15. *Official Records*, ser. 1, vol. 16, pt. 2, 841–42.

16. Ibid., 876.

17. Ibid., 845–46.

18. Ibid., 903–4.

19. Bragg Papers (Western Reserve University, Cleveland, O.), in Connelly, *Army of the Heartland*, 254.

20. Oct. 12, 1862, *Official Records*, ser. 1, vol. 16, pt. 1, 1087.

21. Nov. 9, 1862, Bragg Letters (Special Collections, University of Kentucky, Lexington).

22. J. R. Chumney, Jr., "Don Carlos Buell, Gentleman General" (Ph. D. diss., Rice University, 1964), 182–83; Amos Flegel to parents, Oct. 19, 1962, Flegel Letter (Special Collections, University of Kentucky).

Chapter 4

1. Basil W. Duke, *A History of Morgan's Cavalry* (1867; reprint ed., Bloomington, Ind., 1960), 270.

2. J. M. Porter, "Brief Account of the Experiences of Hon. John M. Porter," (typescript, Kentucky Library), 35.

3. Duke, *Morgan's Cavalry*, 290; Brown, *Bold Cavaliers*, 135.

4. Quoted in Brown, *Bold Cavaliers*, 145–46.

5. Morgan's Report, Jan. 8, 1863, *Official Records*, ser. 1, vol. 20, pt. 1, 156.

6. Dec. 26, 1862, ibid., pt. 2, 243.

7. Duke, *Morgan's Cavalry*, 407, 411.

8. James R. Bentley, ed., "The Civil War Memoirs of Captain Thomas Speed," *The Filson Club History Quarterly* 44 (July 1970):241; John L. Blair, "Morgan's Ohio Raid," ibid., 36 (July 1962):245–49.

9. Brown, *Bold Cavaliers*, 181; Moore's Report, July 4, 1863, *Official Records*, ser. 1, vol. 23, pt. 1, 646.

10. Lewis-Starling Collection; Louisville *Daily Courier*, July 10, 1863.

11. July 11, 22, 1863, Lewis-Starling Collection.

12. Quoted in Brown, *Bold Cavaliers*, 226.

13. Hurlbut to General W. T. Sherman, Mar. 18, 1864, *Official Records*, ser. 1, vol. 32, pt. 3, 91; ibid., pt. 1, 607; Thomas Jordan and J. P. Pryon, *The Campaigns of Lieut.-General Forrest; and of Forrest's Cavalry* (New Orleans, 1868), 409–18.

14. John B. Castleman, *Active Service* (Louisville, 1917), 124.

15. Cecil Fletcher Holland, *Morgan and His Raiders* (New York, 1942), 325.

16. Morgan to General Samuel Cooper, June 11, 1864, *Official Records*, ser. 1, vol. 39, pt. 1, 66.

17. G. D. Ewing, "Morgan's Last Raid into Kentucky," *Confederate Veteran* 31 (July 1923):256.

18. Quoted in Coulter, *Civil War and Readjustment*, 229; July 7, 1862, Wickersham Family Papers (Kentucky Library).

19. A detailed account is L. L. Valentine, "Sue Mundy of Kentucky," *Register of the Kentucky Historical Society* 62 (July and Oct. 1964):175–205, 278–306.

20. Albert Castel, "Quantrill's Missouri Bushwhackers in Kentucky," *The Filson Club History Quarterly* 38 (Apr. 1964):125–32.

21. Collins, *History of Kentucky*, 1:131, 128; Frankfort *Daily Commonwealth*, June 6, 1864.

22. Collins, *History of Kentucky*, 1:142.

23. *Official Records*, ser. 1, vol. 45, pt. 2, 93–94.

24. Duke, *Morgan's Cavalry*, 571, 574–75.

25. Ibid., 577; Basil W. Duke, "Last Days of the Confederacy," *Battles and Leaders* 4:766.

Chapter 5

1. Coulter, *Civil War and Readjustment*, 139–41; Collins, *History of Kentucky*, 1:95; *Congressional Globe*, 37 Cong., 2 sess., pt. 2, Mar. 14, 1862, 1234.

2. *House Journal* (Sept.–Oct. 1861 session), Sept. 5, 1861, 27–34.

3. Ibid. (Aug.–Sept. 1862 session), Aug. 15, 1862, 911, 915.

4. Ibid., Aug. 16, 1862, 929.

5. Frankfort *Tri-Weekly Commonwealth*, Feb. 19, 1863.

6. *Congressional Globe*, 38 Cong., 1 sess., pt. 4, appendix, Mar. 4, 1864, 71.

7. Coulter, *Civil War and Readjustment*, 175.

8. Ibid., 177.

9. Maria Knott to Samuel Knott, Aug. 5, 1863, Knott Collection (Kentucky Library).

10. *Official Records*, ser. 3, vol. 4, 688–90; Louisville *Daily Courier*, Sept. 22, 1864.

11. O. F. Miner to Col. A. M. Stout, Feb. 9, 1865, *Official Records*, ser. 3, vol. 4, 1187–88.

12. Sept. 13, 1861, Robert Anderson Letters (The Filson Club).

13. Boyle to Col. J. B. Fry, *Official Records*, ser. 3, vol. 3, 416.

14. Quoted in Coulter, *Civil War and Readjustment*, 200. William Moody Pratt believed that Bramlette had a nullification document in proof when persuaded not to use it. Pratt Diary, Mar. 21, 1864 (Special Collections, University of Kentucky).

15. *Official Records*, ser. 1, vol. 45, pt. 1, 994; Collins, *History of Kentucky*, 1:148.

16. Message to Congress, Mar. 6, 1862, Basler, ed., *Works of Lincoln*, 5:144–46; Lincoln to Henry J. Raymond, Mar. 9, 1862, ibid., 152–53.

17. Wickersham to father, Feb. 6, 1863, Wickersham Family Papers; Lincoln to Green Adams, Jan. 7, 1863, Basler, ed., *Works of Lincoln*, 6:42.

18. Remarks to Union Kentuckians, Nov. 21, 1862, Basler, ed., *Works of Lincoln*, 5:503–4.

19. Federal Writers' Project, Slave Narratives: Kentucky (Rare Book Room, Library of Congress).

20. Apr. 25, 1862, Joseph I. Younglove Collection; printed form, covering July 1862, Oct. 1863, and Dec. 1864, in Calvert-Obenchain-Younglove Collection (Kentucky Library).

21. Julia Neal, "South Union Shakers during War Years," *The Filson Club History Quarterly* 39 (Apr. 1965):148.

22. *Historical Statistics of the United States* (Washington, D.C., 1949), table L 1-14.

23. J. G. Randall and David Donald, *The Civil War and Reconstruction*, 2d ed. (Boston, 1961), 485; Nov. 28, 1862, Tryon Family Papers (The Filson Club).

24. Quoted in Coulter, *Civil War and Readjustment*, 71.

25. Maury Klein, *History of the Louisville and Nashville Railroad* (New York, 1972), 29–36.

26. *Senate Journal* (Jan.–Mar. 1865 session), Jan. 6, 1865, 11; Collins, *History of Kentucky*, 1:136.

27. Collins, *History of Kentucky*, 1:136.

28. Palmer H. Boeger, "The Great Kentucky Hog Swindle of 1864," *Journal of Southern History* 28 (Feb. 1962):50–70.

29. Frank Pragoff to sister, Oct. 26, 1861, Miscellaneous Papers (The Filson Club).

30. Helen Bartter Crocker, "A War Divides Green River Country," *Register of the Kentucky Historical Society* 70 (Oct.

1972):305; E. R. Weir to Jesse H. Rice, Apr. 24, 1864, in Otto A. Rothert, *A History of Muhlenberg County* (Louisville, 1913), 270; entry for July 27, 1861, John W. Tuttle Diary (Special Collections, University of Kentucky); Maria I. Knott to Sallie Knott, Sept. 26, 1861, Knott Collection; Harriet Means to mother, June 15, 1861, Means Family Papers (Special Collections, University of Kentucky); entry for June 12, 1862, Pratt Diary.

31. Terah W. Sampson to Jerome T. Sampson, Jan. 9, 1862, Terah W. Sampson Letters (The Filson Club).

32. Mrs. Lizzie W. Thomas, typescript of 1894 story in Bowling Green *Times Journal*, Thomas Collection (Kentucky Library); Agatha Strange Journal, 59–60, Strange Collection (Kentucky Library).

33. William P. Davis, Civil War Diary, entries for Sept. 29–Oct. 1, Dec. 14, 1861 (Kentucky Library).

A Note to Readers

Sources on the Civil War in Kentucky are both voluminous and scattered, with libraries and repositories across the country containing collections and occasional items. The footnotes indicate only a few of the sources consulted in the preparation of the manuscript.

One wishing to read on the topic would do well to start with J. G. Randall and David Donald, *The Civil War and Reconstruction*, 2d ed. (Boston, 1961), for an excellent overview of the period and a fine bibliography. For the Kentucky background, Thomas D. Clark, *A History of Kentucky* (Lexington, 1960), is the best starting point, although a number of the older state histories are also helpful. Lewis and Richard H. Collins, *History of Kentucky* (Covington, 1874), 2 vols., contains a great deal of information in the form of undigested annals. Bell I. Wiley in *The Life Of Johnny Reb* (Indianapolis, Ind., 1943), and *The Life of Billy Yank* (Indianapolis, Ind., 1951), has presented the classic description of the life of the common soldier during the Civil War. The best survey of slavery in the state is J. Winston Coleman, Jr., *Slavery Times in Kentucky* (Chapel Hill., N.C., 1940).

Despite its age, E. Merton Coulter, *The Civil War and Readjustment in Kentucky* (Chapel Hill, N.C., 1926; reprint ed., Gloucester, Mass., 1966), remains the best book on the subject. Especially strong on political and economic developments, it is less complete on the military aspects of the war. The Army of Tennessee had a vital role in determining the course of the war in Kentucky; the best study of its campaigns and leaders is

Thomas Lawrence Connelly, *Army of the Heartland* (Baton Rouge, La., 1967) and *Autumn of Glory* (Baton Rouge, La., 1971), although Stanley F. Horn, *The Army of Tennessee* (Indianapolis, Ind., 1941), is still useful. Grady McWhiney, *Braxton Bragg and Confederate Defeat: Field Command* (New York, 1969), is a fine analysis of an unsuccessful commander. Since each is strongly biased, one should balance J. Stoddard Johnston, *Kentucky,* vol. 9 of Clement A. Evans, ed., *Confederate Military History* (Atlanta, Ga., 1899) and Thomas Speed, *The Union Cause in Kentucky, 1860–1865* (New York, 1907), against each other.

The War of the Rebellion: A Compilation of the Official Records of the Union and Confederate Armies, 128 vols. (Washington, D.C., 1880–1901) is an incomparable collection of primary sources—battle reports, letters, telegrams—for both armies; some 30 volumes contain material relating to the war in Kentucky. The naval records, including those for the river gunboats, are in the *Official Records of the Union and Confederate Navies in the War of the Rebellion,* 30 vols. (Washington, D.C., 1894–1922). Robert Underwood Johnson and Clarence Clough Buel, eds., *Battles and Leaders of the Civil War,* 4 vols. (New York, 1887–88) contains a number of articles on the war in Kentucky written by Union and Confederate participants. Perhaps the most interesting personal account by a Kentuckian is Basil W. Duke, *A History of Morgan's Cavalry* (1867; reprint ed., Bloomington, Ind., 1960). Anyone who hopes to understand what the war meant to the soldiers and civilians of that era should read some of the contemporary newspapers and dip into the manuscript collections at such repositories as the libraries of The Filson Club, the State Historical Society, the University of Kentucky and Western Kentucky University.

Minor but nagging questions are often encountered in Civil War reading; many of them can be answered quickly by consulting Mark M. Boatner III, *The Civil*

War Dictionary (New York, 1959). E. B. Long has provided a useful chronology in *The Civil War Day by Day* (New York, 1971), and each Civil War general is discussed briefly in Ezra J. Warner, *Generals in Gray* (Baton Rouge, 1959), and *Generals in Blue* (Baton Rouge, 1964).

Much of the writing on the Civil War in Kentucky has appeared in articles in magazines and historical journals. The *Register of the Kentucky Historical Society* (1903–   ), and *The Filson Club History Quarterly* (1926–   ), contain dozens of such articles, including many edited diaries and collections of letters. Many other magazines and journals also have articles touching upon the Civil War in Kentucky.